Nasar Karim

Myshi Moo and The Frightening Face

Bumblebee Books
London

BUMBLEBEE PAPERBACK EDITION

Copyright © Nasar Karim 2024

The right of Nasar Karim to be identified as author of this work has been asserted in accordance with sections 77 and 78 of the Copyright, Designs and Patents Act 1988.

All Rights Reserved

No reproduction, copy or transmission of this publication may be made without written permission.
No paragraph of this publication may be reproduced, copied or transmitted save with the written permission of the publisher, or in accordance with the provisions of the Copyright Act 1956 (as amended).

Any person who commits any unauthorised act in relation to this publication may be liable to criminal prosecution and civil claims for damage.

A CIP catalogue record for this title is available from the British Library.

ISBN: 978-1-83934-678-1

Bumblebee Books is an imprint of
Olympia Publishers.

First Published in 2024

Bumblebee Books
Tallis House
2 Tallis Street
London
EC4Y 0AB

Printed in Great Britain
www.olympiapublishers.com

Dedication

This book is dedicated to Gemma, Sophia and Aysha.

1

Past the land of trumpet trees, and greedy grass and honeybees, there is a place down a giant hole, where no one ever dares to go. Some say it's a house, some say it's a cave, but no one has ever been so brave, to venture to the horrible hole, so nobody really seems to know. But the story is old and very well known, told to children until they are grown, so they remember to stay close to their homes, and never go out at night alone.

Nobody knows if it's a house or a cave, no one living has been so brave, to venture to the terrible place, and dare to discover the frightening face.

Yes, deep in the hole beyond the trees, there is a face nobody sees, at least not whilst the sun is out, it's a face they only dream about. When the moon is in the sky, and all the people close their eyes, if you should hear a person scream, they might have seen it in a dream. That sad and ghoulish little face, inside that sad and ghoulish place, the strange and dreary, ever so scary, undiscovered living space.

Now, just before the field of flowers, in a town with green clock towers, there is a girl with special powers, her name is Myshi Moo.

She's not the only peculiar child, for many are strange and many are wild, and many have special powers too, but none the same as Myshi Moo. Myshi Moo can dance and sing, and she can draw just about anything, she can write and rhyme and reads just fine, but she's never had what we call bed time.

Being wide awake all hours is Myshi Moo's special power, and can you imagine the things she can do? Twice as much as me or you. Myshi's parents insisted, but Myshi resisted, when they tried to put her to bed at night. Slowly but surely, they lost the fight. They tried songs and stories and long twilight walks, but only stopped worrying once Myshi could talk, and was able to tell them on one of those walks. As they cooed and cajoled by a huge green clock tower, Myshi Moo said, "We've been doing this for hours. Mummy and Daddy I never feel tired, so why don't you two lay down and retire? You get some rest and we'll speak in the morning, I'm rather concerned about your incessant yawning!"

Since the day she was born, she has never once yawned, she's always awake come twilight or dawn. She's seen every minute of every day, she sees them come and go away. She hears the sounds of the day and the night, they used to give her a terrible fright. When the rest of us sleep, she lays in her bed, doing complex equations in her head. She counts at least three hundred sheep, until she knows that we're all asleep. And when the rest of the world is snoring, sometimes Myshi Moo goes exploring.

She knows every corner and each inch of the floor, she knows all the windows and all of the doors. There is nothing unknown and nothing unseen, wherever it is, Myshi has been. There's not a place in the town, she can't navigate, but Myshi Moo has grown frustrated of late. The only things she doesn't yet know, are out in the night, where nobody goes. The only things she hasn't yet seen, are those that can only be seen in dreams. Whilst the rest of the world and the village has slept, her marvellous memory has easily kept, a detailed record of all she has done, but Myshi no longer has any fun.

She's played the same games far too many times, as the

clocks all clicked and night bells chimed. A good conversation helped the hours go by, so Myshi Moo spoke to the moon in the sky. Myshi's sentences stalled, interrupted by sighs, because the moon only listened, and never replied. Her words floated up and nothing came back, her world felt too small, Myshi felt trapped.

After so many long boring nights, Myshi could no longer wait for the light. And with all the time she had on her hands, she developed a theory, and concocted a plan. She slowly put on her warm red coat, and wrote her parents a little note.

"Dear Mummy and Daddy, I've just popped out, there's no need to worry, but you will do no doubt. I won't go too far and I've taken some snacks, and before you know it, I'll be back. I have to explore outside you see, I just want to see the trumpet trees! Have a lovely morning, I'll be home by three, please can I have some chocolate for tea?"

As Myshi stepped out into the dark, in a faraway place, the face did remark. "What is this? It cannot be right. Do I see a child, stepping out in the night?" The buzzy bees buzzed and the trumpet trees swayed, and those who slept were all afraid.

The face saw the end of the endless nights, the land was his until daylight. Nobody had ever left their house in the night, for the long-told tales were probably right. It was far more usual to hear children scream, when they saw the frightening face in their dreams. A little night terror was perfectly all right, but not this, not a person going out at night! All the creatures in the land and the trees, all had a think about what they thought they could see. They were baffled and blinking, all of them thinking, whoever could this little girl be? Whoever could this little girl be?

Even the stars in the night were giddy with glee, a human at night had never been seen. Not since that night so long ago, that had ended down the far away hole. Ever since then, no one came out at night, the story of the hole inspired such fright. And everyone knew about that terrible place, down the terrible hole, and the frightening face. And in the hole, the face came alive, with grinning white teeth and widening eyes. In the town that Myshi was leaving behind, scores of children began to cry. Yes, that was the face's peculiar power, invading dreams around green clock towers. Up jumped the ghoul and more children were shaken, seeing the creature as it did awaken. It's long skinny arms waving around, and from its grinning mouth came such unfamiliar sounds. Hissing and giggling and screaming like wild, the face frightened nearly every child.

Not long after Myshi had left her house to explore, not a child in town was asleep anymore. They'd cried and they'd shouted, and jumped from their beds, rushing to sleep with their parents instead.

As Myshi passed the last clock tower, which even in darkness looked ever so green, she wondered over the next few hours, about all the things she'd never seen. She wondered what she'd find in places, nobody else had even been. The things other children frequently saw, but she had never seen before, for they were only seen when children dreamed, and that was a place Myshi had never been.

From the town she could see grass and trees, and ever so rarely a buzzing bee, but other than rare and distant sightings, she only knew of those things in writing. Beyond the streets of Green Clock Town, all else she knew was written down, in stories and tales that people read, everything else was in Myshi's head. Magical lands and fabulous friends, had kept Myshi company, till it was sunrise again. For over two thousand nights, while all else were in bed, Myshi played with the friends, inside Myshi's head. Endless adventures, and curious creations, but only in

Myshi's imagination.

She'd never slept, she'd never dreamed, she'd never woken with a scream. Devoid of night terrors and frightening visions, Myshi Moo was on a mission. For Myshi Moo was the curious kind, and off she went with a curious mind, with the town full of screams now far behind, Myshi wondered what she would find.

2

The moon hid behind clouds, Myshi felt cold and alone, and every few moments, she wished she'd not left her home. But an hour or so had already passed, and Myshi approached the greedy grass. In the cold lonely night, the grass looked grey, and as Myshi approached, the grass did sway. With a whoosh and a hiss, it moved side to side, and as Myshi drew closer her eyes grew wide.

She'd never seen grass so dense and so tall, from her faraway village it had looked ever so small. For on a clear day, when the sun was bright, you could just see the grass, if conditions were right. But Myshi felt as small as a mouse, the greedy grass was as big as a house. Myshi Moo felt tiny and scared, all because of the stories she'd heard.

But wait! Most of the stories were about the face, in the terrible far off frightening place. The tales of warning said nothing at all, about why the grass was called greedy, or why it was so tall. So as far as Myshi Moo was concerned, there were gaps in the story, and there were things to be learned. Even though she felt awfully frightened, Myshi Moo said "Let us be enlightened." She closed her eyes tight and counted to three, then jumped into the grass and shouted "Whoopeeeee!"

All the clocks atop the green towers, showed three hours past the midnight hour. When the night was dark, and everyone slept, all around town, only ghouls crept. But not on this night, for it was too bright! Yes, though midnight had passed, three hours ago, all the lights in the houses did brightly glow. Every child had woken afraid, and terrible noises most of them made. Crying and yelling, scared out of their heads, they'd all gone running to their parents' beds. Now they were sitting, up late in the night, telling each other about the terrible sights, and the ghastly things that had set them off screaming, now no one was keen, to return to their dreaming.

But in one house in the town, no one said a word, it was eerily quiet, the clocks could be heard. Along with the ticks and the tocks, there wasn't a lot, but the sad sound of two people, who'd just had a shock. They breathed ever so slowly, occasionally gasping, their hearts beating quickly, and one pair of hands, a little note grasping. They both shook their heads and tears fell from their eyes, Myshi Moo's parents had started to cry.

Daddy looked at the words, written in blue, in the lovely handwriting that was Myshi Moo's. He couldn't believe it, and neither could she, their peculiar child, where could she be? What had she been thinking? Wasn't she scared? She'd wandered into the night, that everyone feared! The night full of terrors and terrible unknowns, oh why hadn't Myshi Moo, stayed safe at home?

Myshi's mummy and daddy rushed around in a hurry, their minds were racked with terrible worry. Where could she be, their favourite girl, they loved Myshi Moo more than they loved the whole world. They puzzled and panicked, not quite sure what to do, they had to do something to find Myshi Moo!

3

Myshi lay still, inside the grass, her courage had turned to concern. She cuddled the bag she'd packed with supplies, and said: "There are lessons to learn." But her little legs trembled, as she tried to get up, and all around her was black. No light could enter the greedy grass, Myshi thought she should go back. Back to her house where she knew she was safe, back to her friends with whom she could play. Back to her room with her toys and her books, back to her well-known crannies and nooks. Not so many hours before, Myshi had been certain she had to explore, the unknown night beyond her front door, only a few short hours before. But now she was sad and all in a muddle, all Myshi Moo wanted was her favourite cuddle. It was the cuddle that Mummy and Daddy gave her, she wished Mummy and Daddy would come and save her.

But Myshi Moo knew they would still be at home, and out here in the dark, she was alone. Inside her head she heard Daddy's voice, "whatever is happening, you have a choice." She could choose to give up, be afraid and start crying, or she could get up again, face her fears and keep trying. Whatever it was she'd have to choose it herself, her parents were sleeping like everyone else.

Myshi screwed up her face and slammed her hands on the ground, there was adventure to have and things to be found. Yes, Myshi Moo had had quite enough, she stood up and shouted, "Stupid grass! You're not so tough!"

It may have been anger that made her forget, she'd been frightened a second before, but Myshi was cross, she didn't like being sad, so she chose to be frightened no more. She roared like a bear and threw her fists all around, Myshi Moo was frantically brawling, but after a while, when she ran out of breath, Myshi Moo heard something falling. There was something else, something alive in the grass, and it made an unsettling sound, thousands of 'eeks', and panicking shrieks, Myshi heard thuds on the ground. She whispered "Who's there?" the unsettling sounds were everywhere, a quiet cacophony in the night, something about it didn't seem right.

Myshi's lips trembled, she'd run out of fight, but then she remembered, she had a light! When she'd left her house, she'd had a marvellous thought, along with her snacks, she needed a torch.

"Aha!" she exclaimed as her thumb found the switch, and with the tiniest push, the flashlight went 'click.' There in the grass, she saw an unnatural sight, hundreds of eyes were in the grass that night. They were red eyes and blue eyes, there were purple eyes too, there were green, pink and brown eyes, staring at Myshi Moo.

As Myshi looked closely, she could make out some features, the eyes belonged to some bizarre-looking creatures. They had big faces, small bodies, and long arms and legs, some clung to the grass, some were rubbing their heads. In the unnatural glow Myshi could see, the creatures were brightly coloured and furry. They looked ever so strange, and remarkably cute, but not in the least bit scary. Myshi Moo gave the tiniest wave, keeping her movements slow, she pulled a snack from her bag and held out her hand, nodding she said "There you go."

As the light from the torch kept moving around, Myshi was shocked by the things she had found. They had big round eyes and skinny limbs, plump round bellies and ebony skin, as smooth as silk and glistening. Their arms and their legs and their backs and their heads, were covered in the silkiest threads, fur that looked so wonderfully combed, in a variety of the most marvellous tones.

Her big hazel eyes were met by theirs, hundreds of startled little stares. Not one of the funny beings dared move, Myshi said "what on earth are you?"

All at once the creatures whispered, with voices like the breeze "Why, we are the creatures that hide in the grass, the creatures that nobody sees."

As the chorus rose into endless night, creating a certain suspense, to Myshi Moo something didn't seem right, something didn't make sense. Just like everyone else, Myshi Moo knew, the grass was considered out of bounds, 'the greedy grass' everyone called it, but what had Myshi Moo found? With a name like that, the greedy grass, had a fearsome reputation, but it was full of cute creatures, that couldn't be right, she needed an explanation.

So as the creatures stared at Myshi Moo, with hundreds of colourful eyes, Myshi wondered what she should say, and what might the creatures reply. "Why" she wondered, would they live, inside the greedy grass? Maybe they were not aware, that they really shouldn't trespass. Was it possible that no one had ever suggested, that the creatures might soon be ingested?

Myshi Moo's mind worked double time, that's twice as

fast as yours or mine, and as she was hypothesising, a terrible thing she was realising. There were so many creatures in the grass, judging by numbers they had clearly thrived, could they have given the grass its grave reputation, could that be the reason they had survived? Inside Myshi's little head, came an idea full of dread, what if the furry little beasts, were going to have a Myshi feast? The countless faces seemed to grin, like gargoyles in the night, and in their jaws their fangs did sparkle, glinting in the moving light.

But many lonely nights had taught her, that she must always control her thinking, or her head could quickly fill with nonsense, and she would find herself sinking. Myshi Moo stared straight ahead, she knew she had a choice, so she decided to ignore the fear, and concentrate on her voice. She pulled back her shoulders and stuck out her chin, she kept her voice measured and low, trying to sound friendly and calm, she started with a friendly "Hello!"

All the creatures were silent, at the peculiar child they gazed, their big kaleidoscope colourful eyes, all looked rather amazed. They'd never had a visitor like this, no one friendly ever came to the grass, so it's easy to see why the poor little things, might all be feeling aghast.

Myshi continued, she was not fazed, again she spoke and again they gazed.

"My name is Myshi Moo, isn't the world quite lovely tonight, how do all of you do?"

The creatures still did not respond, though they understood every word, it was simply that a human being, being in the grass seemed utterly absurd. Humans had feared them for time untold, and always left them well alone, and as for all the non-human beings, they would all be eaten, skin flesh and bones. Whoever had gone into the grass, had either been eaten or ran away very fast. But this little girl seemed to be unaware, either that or she did not feel fear.

Many years earlier, before Myshi's parents were babies, two hundred plombidonks had been seen by a lady. Now plombidonks were beautiful birds, blessed with the most beautiful feathers, and on that day a lady had seen, hundreds all flying together. They circled the tall grass that grew outside the town, then all at once they all flew down, a spectacle of grace and plombidonk song, but it was all over forever before very long. The lady was stunned, it was a glorious sight, but what happened next, gave the lady a fright. The plombidonks song became a symphony of screams, and that was the last time they'd ever been seen. For the poor plombidonks had gone to feast on the grass, it was easily the best in the land, they thought it was full of fat worms and bugs, upon which to feast they had planned. The grass concealed fantastical flowers, and the plombidonks had reckoned, they'd eat those flowers and then take a rest, and have the worms and bugs for seconds. But the hungry plombidonks plan, lacked one crucial feature, they had no idea that the grass, contained some ravenous creatures.

When all the birds had disappeared, the watching lady did despair, she threw her hands into the sky, and running back to town she cried. "The grass the grass, it ate the birds, it ate the plombidonks! The grass the grass it ate them all, I heard it crunch and chomp!" The lady shouted in the streets, beneath the green clock towers, she told all the people in the town, how the plombidonks had been devoured. Every man, woman and child, gathered to hear the lady, some were amused, but most were afraid, and the rest just thought she was crazy. Before too long all of the people and some animals as well, had all listened to the frightened lady, with the frightful tale to tell. She pulled her hair and wrung her hands and shakily she said, "The grass ate them all! You must believe me! The grass is ferocious, the grass is greedy!"

That was many years ago, and ever since that time, no human had been near the grass, and the creatures liked that fine. The furry things with colourful eyes within the grass remained concealed, and the birds and beasts that came along were all turned into meals.

For generations since that time, the eating of birds so gruesome and gory, many people in green clock tower town, had heard the gruesome plombidonk story. But not a single person knew, about the furry little beings, that Myshi Moo had stumbled upon, and she currently stood there seeing. The greedy grass, the trumpet trees, the scary face and the buzzing bees, Myshi Moo had not a clue, whether any of it was actually true.

So far you see no one had asked, about the true nature of the greedy grass. And certainly none had ever been, as far as the fabled trumpet trees. Now Myshi was too scared to ask, why it was called the greedy grass. She'd stumbled in too far and too swiftly, to extricate herself quietly or quickly. She wondered if she could retreat, before she became something to eat. Again she thought she should have stayed home, and the creatures were having thoughts of their own. For centuries they'd been left alone! But now their whereabouts were known.

For that night a human did intrude, into their blissful solitude. And most of the many fuzzaroos, for that was their proper name, had never seen a real human being, for humans never came. The fuzzaroos had run from humans, who hunted them for their skin, with which they made the warmest clothes, and wigs to look pretty in. So many distant aeons ago, the fuzzaroos found the tallest grass, to hide from humans forever more, and live in peace at last. But on this unprecedented night, into their world a human came, the fuzzaroos wondered if they'd be skinned and eaten, and Myshi Moo wondered the same.

Everyone and everything, in the blue and black and grey, held their breath as the torch light shone, and the grass did quietly sway. The moon itself was watching, wondering what would happen next, and then deep inside the greedy grass, Myshi Moo took a little step. The fuzzaroos seemed to grow larger, as their fur stood up on end, they were terrified and so was Myshi, but Myshi Moo tried to pretend. She hid her fear behind a smile and took a few deep breaths, then in her softest, gentlest, friendliest voice, she repeated some of what she'd said. "Hello creatures, I'm Myshi Moo, what a beautiful night, who are you?"

This time there came an answer, Myshi did not see who'd spoken, she looked around at all the faces, relieved the silence had been broken.

"Well, hello Myshi Moo, we are the fuzzaroos." A peculiar shadowy silhouette came closer to Myshi Moo, she raised her torch and saw red ruby eyes and fur that was brilliant bright blue. The blue fuzzaroo tapped his shiny shoe, three times on the ground, all the others in the grass, gingerly jumped down. Quickly and quietly they gathered, all around their visitor, and the furry blue red eyed one, became Myshi Moo's inquisitor.

"How do you do, Miss Myshi Moo? Why have you come to our home? We don't want to be rude Miss Myshi Moo, why can't you leave us alone? It really is a little strange, wouldn't you agree, for a human being to come to the grass, after what must be centuries?" Myshi was a little startled, she wasn't sure what to say, but the fuzzaroo didn't wait for answers and carried on anyway.

"Don't you know for many years, we fuzzaroos lived in the trees, but humans destroyed our habitat, they would not let us be. We were chased from all of our favourite places, driven from our homes, you horrible humans wanted our fur, and chewed the meat from our bones!"

The fuzzaroo spoke louder and faster, he was very animated, Myshi wished he'd stop or slow down, she waited and she waited.

"Big beasts eat the little ones, and you're higher up the chain, but you greedy humans just hunt and keep hunting, till nothing else remains!"

Myshi was bewildered by the ranting fuzzaroo, he waved his little arms around, whilst Myshi wondered what to do.

"This grass! This wonderful tall and luscious grass, is our final hiding place, you humans ruined everywhere else, this is the only place that's safe. What do you mean by coming here, what do you think you're doing? I'll tell you this my little friend, there is danger brewing. And if you think you're going to take our fur, to make a brightly coloured cape, the fuzzaroos will destroy you, little girl there's no escape!"

At last the fuzzaroo stopped shouting, Myshi took a breath, but before she could say a single word, the fuzzaroos all shouted "Death!"

Every single fuzzaroo was wearing fancy shoes, and they were all walking with their hands outstretched, towards a panicked Myshi Moo. Their brilliant eyes seemed mad with greed, and they all grinned a dreadful grin, their lips pulled back across their jaws, revealing terrible teeth within. Every mouth contained two rows of razor -sharp incisors; Myshi nearly collapsed with fear, but knew no one would revive her. Poor Myshi Moo felt quite awful, eating her would be unlawful, but the law was not her greatest worry, she had to do something in a hurry. The fuzzaroos were going to eat her, though they were quite adorable, they bared their teeth and it was clear, their intentions were deplorable. Even though Myshi was afraid, she thought it wiser to be brave, she filled her little lungs with air then made the loudest noise she'd ever made.

"RAAAAAAAAAAAAAAAAAAAAAAA!" she roared a mighty roar and the fuzzaroos were shocked, they covered their ears with their little hands and in their tracks they stopped. Myshi saw her plan was working and ran towards the beasts, who only seconds earlier had planned a Myshi feast. As Myshi screamed and beat her chest, like a big angry gorilla, the fuzzarros became convinced she was a ferocious killer. She grabbed the king of the fuzzaroos, with his bright blue fur and bright red shoes, she lifted him and held him high, with his bottom pointing at the sky.

Initially her plan had been, to bang her chest a lot and scream, so the fuzzaroos would be afraid, but that was all the plan she'd made. Myshi had thought she must be doomed, but then, beneath the bright blue moon, as she held her hostage high, the fuzzaroos began to cry. Whilst she'd escaped a ghastly fate, and saved herself from dinner plates, she certainly had not been trying to bring about such woeful crying. As carefully as she could move, she lowered the bright blue fuzzaroo, and placed him gently on his feet, but even he began to weep. He looked up with his ruby eyes, they were wide with fear, Myshi pulled a napkin from her pocket, and wiped away his tears. The frightened little fuzzaroo sobbed uncontrollably. Myshi spoke to him softly, saying "don't be scared of me." Myshi Moo felt pangs of guilt, she had not meant to cause any trouble, she knelt beside the trembling fuzzaroo and gave him a calming cuddle. Seeing her wrap him in her arms, caused the other fuzzaroos alarm, they thought that she might cause him harm, and what do you think they did?

The fuzzaroos began to sing, "Please oh please don't eat our King, and we will give you anything, but spare our mighty King. Please spare our royal Ragaboo, leader of the fuzzaroos, don't harm his highness Ragaboo, leader of the fuzzaroos."

Myshi felt a little bad, for making the fuzzaroos so sad, but of not being eaten she was glad, and now the upper hand she had.

Myshi knew the fuzzaroos would now do what she said they must, as long as she could first of all, win the fuzzaroo's trust. She thought she could be their new best friend, if they thought she'd saved them from the end. She helped poor Ragaboo to his feet, then carefully began to speak.

"Fuzzaroos your king is safe, and I won't be eating you

today, though you all look very tempting, very tasty I must say!" Myshi stuck out her little chin and flared her nostrils just a bit, making sure she looked quite menacing, as the torch her grizzly grimace lit. She gave her torch a sudden wave, to check the fuzzaroos were afraid. She saw a trembling in their knees, and Myshi Moo felt rather pleased.

"Listen to me fuzzaroos, I am the mighty Myshi Moo, and if you're good, here's what I'll do, I'll make sure no harm comes to you!" All the fuzzaroos clung on, to every word she said, the plan so far seemed to be working, as she filled their little heads. The plan was to find the frightening face, to see what was in dreams at last, but first she must escape this place, the treacherous greedy grass. As Myshi Moo had never slept, she could not really empathise, with people who were all of afraid, of a face she had not seen with her eyes.

The fuzzaroos had formed a circle, all around the Mighty Moo, they looked at her with frightened awe, while Myshi wondered what to do. She reached into her bag, and filled her hands with treats, then in a mighty voice she boomed "Fuzzaroos I bring you sweets!"

The fuzzaroos froze and waited, they all held their fuzzaroo breath, the King of fuzzaroos took a sweet, and courageously performed a royal test. He placed the sweet inside his mouth, and sucked majestically for a while, before too long he nodded his head, and smiled his royal smile. King Ragaboo held one hand aloft, and with a loud gulp he swallowed, Myshi Moo was not prepared for the mania that followed.

Before she know what was going on, she was overrun by fuzzaroos, it was a frantic mass of silky fur, and sparkly colourful shoes. Myshi fell onto her back, the fuzzaroos were having so much fun, they found every single treat she had, and ate every single one. When the feeding frenzy ended, Myshi was down but was not beaten, she lay laughing in the long soft grass, because she knew she wouldn't be eaten.

Her monumental victory filled Myshi Moo with pride, despite having been very frightened, she was glad to be outside. And once again she heard a voice, it spoke inside her head, something Myshi's daddy told her, before he'd gone to bed. "Whatever happens Myshi Moo, you can decide what you must do."

She missed her mummy and daddy too, as she lay smiling on the floor, but she was still extremely happy, that she'd chosen to ignore, all the stories and warnings, about the greedy grass, everyone knew those scary stories, but now she knew the truth at last! There were many parables, told for generations, and as nobody had tested them, they needed investigation. The greedy grass had for so long, inspired so much fear, and it turned out all those frightened people, all had the wrong idea. None of the stories had ever mentioned, the existence of the fuzzaroos, and everyone had overlooked, the realities of what grass can do.

Myshi told her brand-new friends, how everyone she knew, had not the faintest inkling, about the fuzzaroos. She told her new acquaintances, the people all believed, if they went into the greedy grass, they would never leave. For certainly they would be eaten, that's why the grass had grown so tall, the people thought the greedy grass, would eat them one and all.

The fuzzaroos were all enthralled and really quite

amused, "Myshi Moo" said Ragaboo, "we're all rather confused. Pleased we are that they are scared, and at the same time entertained, for we thought human beings were clever, why don't they use their brains?"

The conversation carried on, with both sides contributing, there was laughter and there was fascination, and even some disputing. Myshi felt more wide awake than she could remember feeling, of course she'd always been awake, but the night so far had been revealing. She'd learnt more since leaving her cosy home, than any human before had known, certainly about one thing at least, and she'd discovered an unknown type of beast; the fuzzaroos and their colourful King, who loved to eat sweets and loved to sing, and more importantly than any of that, she knew the grass didn't eat a thing. It was just a mistake, a misconception, it seemed quite funny on reflection, for so many people had been living in terror, all because of a silly error.

4

Back inside the house of Moo, after discussing for some time, Myshi's father had agreed, to leave green clock tower town behind. He could not find his torch, beyond the town there was meagre light, but Mr Moo went into the dark, for the one thing he wanted was out in the night.

At the door he paused and turned, and looked at his worried wife, he could see his missing daughter, in her mother's eyes.

"I'll find her and I'll bring her back" Mrs Moo did not reply, but she smiled as well she was able, then she kissed Mr Moo goodbye. From the door she watched her husband, walk away from home, towards the fields, towards the trees, towards the things unknown.

Mrs Moo felt all alone, but she'd decided to stay at home, in case her daughter re-appeared, whilst her husband was gone. She wondered why her little girl, who she loved more than the world, would want to go towards the trees, where goodness knew what there might be. But in her heart she'd half expected, she felt that maybe she'd neglected, her little girl who now was gone, felt she might have done something wrong. For how could a mind like Myshi Moo's, ever find enough to do, she knew how much her girl could do, twice as much as me or you.

She'd known that her peculiar child, who'd never needed to slumber, would one day need to go outside, into the night and wander.

Mr Moo walked rapidly, through the fields of flowers in the dark, and just as it had a few hours before, the frightening face remarked.

"Again I see, it can't be true, out at night, not one but two, people out at night I see, why and how, what can this be?" He tilted his head, and looked ever so ghoulish, "People out in the dark, ever so foolish!" They had left their sanctuaries, to enter his domain, "But the night is mine, the night is mine!" growled the frightening face in vain. The frightening face scrunched up his nose, in angry irritation, what was the scariest way he wondered, to deal with the situation. He drummed the ground with his toes, with his long pale fingers he scratched his head, "I'll stay out of dreams the rest of this night, and watch these wanderers instead."

As Myshi left, the fuzzaroos danced, singing their goodbyes, Myshi looked at the horizon askance, surveying the deep dark sky. The night so far had been eventful indeed, Myshi wondered what else she might see, she realised she'd have to pick up some speed, as she'd promised her parents she'd be home for tea.

Familiar words from tales old, crept into Myshi's mind, as she continued through the endless night, in the pale moonshine.

"The trumpet trees, the trumpet trees, a stranger tree there's never been. If you ever see the trumpet trees, remember that you must flee. For if you ever hear their sound, your little head will spin around, your little ears will seal your fate, and you will never ever be found.

"If you ever hear the trumpet trees, the terrible blast of

trumpet trees, don't stop to listen, don't stop to think, if you have a chance then you must flee, run far away from the trumpet trees."

Myshi could not turn it off, her thoughts could not drown it out, at first she'd heard only a whisper, but now the words seemed to shout. Myshi stopped and looked behind her, was it true they'd never find her? Would she never go back to her home, was she always going to be alone? Myshi began to feel afraid, she thought about her friends, what if Myshi saw the trees, but never saw her town again? The little town with green clock towers, her toys and her books, the field of flowers. What if she never got her tea? That would be a catastrophe!

Myshi's eyes had long adjusted, she could clearly see into the night, but Myshi wasn't sure she trusted, the things that seemed to be in sight. In her peculiar predication, Myshi realised her situation, might just be a manifestation, of something called hallucination. Myshi wished the song would stop, and as she did the penny dropped, it might just be her imagination, might just be a hallucination. Hallucinations she'd recently read, were usually created inside our heads, utterly real they looked and sounded, but factually they were unfounded.

Myshi made some silly noises, then sang along in ridiculous voices, trying hard to make fun of the song, and rather quickly the voice was gone. Once again the night was quiet and Myshi wandered on her own, a peculiar child with peculiar powers, wandering far from home.

Mr Moo stood perfectly still, he'd not been walking long at all, but only a few more steps ahead, was the greedy grass, so thick and so tall. The grass stood like a giant sentry, wide and strong forbidding entry. As a child Mr Moo had learned, that if you entered the grass you never returned.

But Mr Moo had found a path, beyond the town with green clock towers, familiar footprints in the grass, he'd followed them for nearly an hour. Now he stood far from home, Myshi's footprints besides his own, and they led into the greedy grass, into the great unknown. He thought about his wife at home, he knew she was waiting there, he trembled before the greedy grass, Myshi's trail had brought him here. The grass about which they'd all been warned, but what if his little Myshi had gone, into the grass earlier that night, for it had a deadly appetite. His little girl, his whole wide world, he loved everything about her, and into the grass he knew he must go, because he knew he could not be without her.

He narrowed his eyes and reached out with both hands, grabbing and pulling the grass apart, he reluctantly put forward one foot and stepped, from the night into the dark.

5

It wasn't too long before little Myshi, was totally absorbed in the sounds of the night, apart from the crunching and tap of her feet, there were strange sounds of animals and marvellous sights. It was as if everything had turned down its glow, to blend into the twilight shadows. The sky up above was full of strange hues, ghostly whites, spectral purples and blues. It was like nothing Myshi had seen before, it was so much more magical than being indoors. For the first time Myshi Moo could recall, the things that bothered her didn't matter at all. For most of her life, Myshi Moo had been keen, to know what it was like to dream. Sometimes people would awake, and recount fantastical adventures, they'd been far away with magical creatures, in a land that Myshi could never enter. A land where animals talked and people could fly, and you could even play with old friends who had died. It was a land where each person had wonderful powers, whilst all Myshi had were green clock towers, and empty rooms and lonely hours.

    Now clouds across the night sky jaunted, and the wind its ghostly singing flaunted, Myshi came to feeling daunted, for the strangest silhouette she could see. Against a backdrop of deep grey, a group of giants seemed to sway, with countless arms all on display, against the deep dark grey.

    Myshi Moo was mesmerised, what was this thing

before her eyes, taking Myshi by surprise, above the earth it seemed to rise.

Then it hit her suddenly, Myshi knew what she could see, the only thing that it could be, Myshi was looking at the trumpet trees! Like writhing serpents branches sprawled, their dance held Myshi Moo enthralled, and eerie voices seemed to call, "come to the trumpet trees."

The voices seemed to wrap around her, like a silky trap that did surround her, in deep twilight, they had found her, they were the trumpet trees.

The trumpet trees you may be aware, tended to inspire fear, but no one had ever stopped to explain, how or why they got their name.

As towards the trees she seemed to float, Myshi made a mental note, 'I don't know the trumpet trees, and they certainly don't know me. What's so bad about the trees? Let's just go and see.'

Myshi Moo had reached the trees, it didn't take too long, it all happened by itself, she'd been transported by the song. She patted her limbs and checked her things, straightening her hair, could it be that these strange trees, might be trumpeters?

"It's not impossible" thought Myshi Moo, for who had ever known, that the creatures known as fuzzaroos had made the grass their home. Myshi could not ascertain, from where the voice was emanating, she felt marvellously entertained, these trees were fascinating. Could the trees be like the grass, filled with little beings, or would Myshi be surprised again, by whatever she'd be seeing?

6

Stepping slowly Mr Moo, remembered what he had to do, for he was frightened of the grass, but it was the grass he must go through. He closed his eyes and held his breath, half expecting certain death, but maybe his Myshi was inside, he gulped and took a heavy stride. The grass was taller than Mr Moo, it looked like it would eat him whole, but he was sure his child had been through, so he knew he had to go. With his eyes still closed, he imagined his wife, all alone for the rest of her life, he imagined his baby, his marvellous child, never being found, disappeared in the wild. There could be nothing more dreadful than losing his Myshi Moo, and for Mrs Moo it might be worse, for she might lose her husband too.

"But this is all silliness and speculation," said Mr Moo in a confident voice "A thing like this requires investigation, whatever is happening I have a choice."

Mr Moo walked purposefully, he felt the grass all around, a whole minute passed and he was still alive, maybe even safe and sound. He rubbed his eyes and looked around, but there was not a thing to see, just darkness and grass in all directions, "Oh where on earth could Myshi Moo be?" He called her name but no reply, came to him in the night, he looked around harder, that was no use, grass was the only sight. He knew the footprints he had followed belonged to Myshi Moo, but her trail had been entirely swallowed, maybe he would be swallowed too. Mr Moo would not give up, there was far too much at stake, he absolutely must find Myshi, whatever it might take. Finding his child was his chief concern, though he still thought he might be devoured, he would never allow himself to fail, just because he'd been a coward.

"Myshi! My Myshi! Where are you it's Daddy!" He shouted into the grassy abyss, and then from all around came an unusual voice, and the unusual voice said this.

"Who dares to enter this magical grass, it is forbidden for mankind! If you don't want to be eaten, leave at once! No Myshi in the grass you will find!"

Mr Moo was furious, his blood began to boil. His lungs filled up with angry air, he slammed his boots into the soil. How dare the grass be so bold, Mr Moo would not be told, not by the grass, or me or you, that he'd not find his Myshi Moo. He'd find his Myshi Moo, he knew, and if it took him hundred years, then he'd still find his Myshi Moo, he would not let her disappear!

He howled and growled, like a monster unchained, he seemed both dangerous and deranged. The fuzzaroos were hidden, they all looked at their king, then the bravest said to Ragaboo, "You've got to do something." He shrugged his shoulders up and down, the fuzzaroos were scared, he had no idea what he should do, he was utterly unprepared. Mr Moo was twice as loud and large as Myshi Moo, the fuzzaroos might have to attack, if he was not subdued. The King raised his arms and filled his chest despite his empty head, then in his most commanding voice, this is what he said.

"Oh what a noise, oh what a racket, oh what a din you

make, clearly you are agitated, calm down for goodness sake."

Mr Moo stopped his screaming, and looked in all directions. "Who's that?" he said. "Who said that?" he shouted with an angry red complexion.

"It is I," continued Ragaboo, "the beast that rules this world, and as I am mighty and omniscient, I know you seek the girl."

Daddy Moo's eyes were glowing with rage, the blood was racing in his veins, "Where's my little girl?" he screamed, sounding quite insane.

The fuzzaroos quietly wooed, at this new piece of information, the mad man was Myshi Moo's father, now this was a revelation. Maybe he had sweets as well, but he seemed less gregarious, if the fuzzaroos made one false move, things could get quite serious. The King knew that he must think fast, to protect the fuzzaroos and the grass. The fuzzaroos could rather easily, eat the angry man, he looked rather large and rather tasty, but the King dismissed that plan. For he knew that there would be trouble, if ever they ate a person, other people would invade their bubble, and then things would surely worsen. Mr Moo would certainly taste good and eating him would be fun, but once he was inside their bellies the damage could not be undone. As well as that the king decided, the fuzzaroos might feel quite bad, they'd all quite liked the little girl, so they probably shouldn't eat her dad.

So he came up with another plan, a plan to calm the human down, and make sure there were no more visits, from people in green clock tower town.

"Your child is safe," the king continued, "though she

would have made a tasty snack, but we've just eaten a hundred parrots, so we made Myshi promise she won't come back!"

"She was here!" he gasped ecstatically, so happy to hear the news. "She was here?" he asked, just to be sure, "My little Myshi Moo?"

"Yes indeed, the child who came, a short while before you, was certainly the one you seek, her name was Myshi Moo."

"How do you know that it was her, are you absolutely sure? What did she say? What did she look like, this little girl you saw?"

"She was very strange, as you all are, very pretty for a human being, a red coat she had and big hazel eyes, with which to do her human seeing. Her hair was brown, with golden hues, she said her name was Myshi Moo. She was well behaved for a human being, and remarkably polite, but whatever the case two human beings, is too many for one night!" The King had tried to sound ominous and send the man off running, but he seemed to miss the obvious, and the questions kept on coming.

"How could you see the colour of her hair and her eyes in the middle of the night, and how could you tell her coat is red, when there is hardly any light?" By now the king of fuzzaroos was quite exasperated, so in his deepest most majestic voice, the following he stated. "Enough Mr Moo, you try my patience, I grow tired of your questions, now if you ever wish to see your child, you should follow my suggestion. I suggest you leave the grass at once, for too much time has passed, since a tasty crunchy human being was eaten by the grass!

Myshi Moo has left the grass, she went towards the trees, and you must follow or you'll be eaten, on the count of twenty -three."

The grass in front of Mr Moo, began to separate, it seemed to magically come apart, creating a path for him to take. Then all at once, the grass had eyes, green, red, blue and pink, Mr Moo was terrified, he didn't stop to think. The booming voice had started counting and was already on number eight, there were only fifteen seconds left, for Mr Moo to escape. The King continued counting, and all the fuzzaroos, began to laugh like maniacs, watching Mr Moo. Their laughter echoed in his head, and the King reached twenty -three, but just before he got there, Mr Moo was free.

7

The darkness seemed darker than it had been before, where there had only been night there seemed to be more. All alone sat Mrs Moo, with no idea of what to do. Not even knowing whether or when, she'd ever see her family again. The house was empty, the house was no fun, without Myshi up at all hours, she wished her husband and daughter would come, to the town with green towers. Her peculiar child, her one of a kind, who'd gone out in the night, and left her losing her mind.

What if she waited and waited, and Myshi never came home, she'd just have been waiting, to spend her life all alone. What if she followed her into the night, only to disappear, and her husband and daughter returned to the house, and found nobody there?

It seemed that whatever she did, she'd be in a terrible way, she thought she mustn't go out, and thought she mustn't stay. Her home was a prison, and her mind was the lock, but there was no key, just the ticking of clocks.

Myshi lay on the ground feeling quite surprised, the trumpet tree branches she had realised, were more like an army of arms and hands, and they could stretch like enormous rubber bands. It wasn't just branches of the trumpet trees, that were unlike anything she'd ever seen, the trees themselves were just as unique, they didn't just stand there, they could think, sing and speak!

Carried by branches and laid on the ground, Myshi went into a stupor, marvelling at the trumpet trees voices, the experience was really quite super. The voices asked Myshi if she'd like to rest, Myshi Moo wondered, what would be best. What would be wise and what would be fun, she was no longer frightened, so there was no need to run. She could lie forever in the magical tree, but she'd promised her parents she'd be home for tea.

The trumpet trees were holding court, and Myshi Moo believed she aught, to be polite for she was a guest, and she felt like she'd benefit from taking a rest. The trumpet tree branches were supple and soft, they'd lifted Myshi and held her aloft, and placed her ever so gently down, and the trumpet trees were all around.

Myshi Moo had expected to see, trumpets sticking out of the trees, or at least a tree that made trumpeting sounds, but that was not what she had found. For from it in fact the trees were just trees, though unlike any she'd ever imagined or seen. They were tall and dark and ever so smooth, and as you already know the branches could move. The trees could talk, the trees could sing, but their name really had Myshi Moo wondering. Not long ago she'd been frightened and awed, as the trumpet tree branches had become the floor. The whole world around her had seemed to be moving, singing trees, moving branches, it had been very confusing.

The trees seemed pleased, to have Myshi there, for they had stood undisturbed for countless years. That's why they had sung and told her to come, and now she was there they were all having fun. The magical branches all seemed quite keen, to entertain a human being. They made sure she was cosy and played with her hair, and whilst she was still confused, she was glad to be there. Myshi giggled a little at the whole situation, in only one night she'd found some marvellous creations. She was keen to resolve her current confusion, and the trees certainly seemed not to mind the intrusion.

"May I ask a question," said Myshi Moo softly, "there's something that's confusing me. Everyone I've ever spoken to, says you're called the Trumpet trees."

"What's confusing about that? That's what we are called, it makes absolute sense, and that really is all."

"Well I don't see a trumpet, so I don't agree, why are you called the trumpet trees?"

The branches around her had all been playing, they all stopped to hear what Myshi was saying. The whole world around, now seemed to be staring at her, the leaves did not rustle, the breeze did not stir. Myshi began to feel a touch of unease, at being surrounded by tall silent trees. Myshi could feel her heart beating faster, and she wondered what she had done, she felt a sense of impending disaster, and she knew there was nowhere to run.

The night was dark the silence immense, Myshi felt trapped in the forest so dense. She thought she could feel a ball in her lungs, it was hard to breathe, she wasn't sure what she'd done. Though she was curious and brave and remarkably smart, she began to feel like she was falling apart. She was alone and afraid in an unknown place, and though she tried to act normal, it showed on her face.

Her little lips trembled and she let out a squeak, she

blinked and a tear, rolled down her cheek. Once again the branches shook, slowly at first then faster and faster, the silence that had so unnerved Myshi Moo, was replaced by a monstrous laughter. It was guttural and deep, it made the ground shake, at first Myshi thought it was an earthquake. It grew louder and louder, she thought the trees had gone mad, but the laugh was infectious, and she no longer felt sad. In fact she stopped crying, as the world wobbled like jelly, and she began laughing so hard, she had to hold on to her belly.

The trees held up their branches, and begged each other to stop, if they hadn't been rooted and so close together, they might have laughed till they dropped. If they hadn't been trees they'd have rolled around on the ground, Myshi covered her ears to block out the sound. When she'd managed to stop herself laughing along, in her most serious voice she boomed "What's going on?"

A nearby tree, in between giggles and shrieks, wiped tears from its trunk and started to speak. "Well, you ask why we're called trumpet trees, you seem so confused by the things that you see, poor little girl, oh deary me!"

"Well you don't play trumpets, make trumpets, or look like them either, so why you're called trumpet trees I cannot decipher."

"You humans expect to understand everything, but that's not how it works, where shall we begin?"

The trumpet trees laughed for a few moments more, but not quite as hard, as they had done before. "You arrogant beings always believe, you're all far too clever to be deceived. But you fool yourselves with your words and your eyes, and when things don't make sense, you tell yourselves lies."

"Well" replied Myshi "I'm a human being, and your name doesn't match with what I am seeing! So I think it's rather silly and mean, making rude comments about human beings."

"Oh sweet little girl, no offence is intended, if your feelings are hurt, let's get them mended. You see, we trees, we've been called different names, but what we do is always the same. We were here before humans, before dinosaurs too, and when your time is up, can you guess what we do?"

"When my time is up, what do you mean?"

"Not just your time Myshi Moo, we mean all human beings?"

"All human beings, people everywhere?"

"Yes, all human beings, will one day disappear."

"You mean we'll go to the angels? I already know, my mummy and daddy, already said so. So that's not a surprise, that's old news to me, but you still haven't explained, why you're called trumpet trees."

The largest tree, opened its eyes, taking Myshi Moo by surprise. The tree's eyes looked old, understanding and kind "One day Myshi Moo, you'll leave this world behind."

"Hang on a second!" Myshi exclaimed "You called me Myshi Moo! How do you know my name?"

"Oh, we know everyone's name, we've been here since time began, and we'll be here till the end, it's all part of the plan."

The trees had Myshi's full attention, she wanted to

know the plan, she stared at the trees with her hazel eyes, and held the branches with little hands.

The trees were wondering what to do, they'd never have spoken to me or you, they'd often been silent for millions of years, but they'd chosen to speak to Myshi Moo. Myshi Moo was one of a kind, the trees knew all too well, a peculiar child with a marvellous mind, so the trees decided to tell.

"Myshi Moo, you have no dreams, we know you never sleep, so I'll tell you things no dreamer knows, a secret you must keep. We know you know about the grass, and you met the fuzzaroos, we know you have heard of the buzzy bees, and the frightening face is waiting for you."

"Will I be safe?" she asked the trees. "Why is the face waiting for me?"

"Whatever will happen will happen my dear, you'll have to wait and see."

"That's a stupid answer" Myshi Moo thought, but decided not to speak out, she desperately wanted the tress to tell her, what the plan was all about.

"Everyone knows we are trumpet trees, but nobody can tell you why, because they will only learn the reason, just before they..."

"Just before what?" Myshi cried.

"Just before they die."

An eerie quietness fell upon and all around the trees, Myshi Moo asked them shakily, "What's going to happen to me?"

Her breath became a nebulous cloud, floating in the night, her heart seemed to skip several beats, her head was feeling light. Myshi's breathing accelerated, the trees did not reply, Myshi's lips began trembling again, and she blinked her hazel eyes. She feared what she had just been told, she wasn't even quite old, she thought she might be about to cry, she wondered if this meant she was going to die.

The ground became a quiet commotion, with branches moving like an ocean, rising in a leafy flurry, and the tree said, "Myshi Moo don't worry. Wipe the tears from your face, you'll leave this place." The moving branches had formed a ball, a few Myshis wide and two Myshis tall, it was like a like an arboreal igloo, built around Myshi Moo.

"There's no need to cry, no need to scream, just pretend this is a dream. A special gift from the trumpet trees, now listen very carefully. You know you're absolutely right, there's not a single trumpet in sight, and we'll tell you this so you're not afraid, you won't be seeing one tonight.

From these trees there comes a blast, only when a time has passed, the loudest blast you ever hear, and soon after that, you disappear. But you won't hear a blast my dear, and certainly will not disappear. The blasts are like a trumpet blowing, and all who hear it are wiped out, without the next world ever knowing, what our name is all about. The next trumpet blast will be number five, the last four blasts not a soul survived. And a brand- new world replaced those ones, until the end of this world comes.

Now great adventure lies ahead, and you must never repeat what we have said."

The trees stood still, the moon was gleaming, Myshi wondered if she'd been dreaming. The forest was just as it should be, a normal forest, with normal trees. Only the sounds Myshi Moo should encounter, in an ordinary forest did surround her. Whatever had happened was wonderful, whether or not it had happened at all.

Myshi pulled her coat, around her a little tighter, after all the things she'd seen that night, Myshi was feeling a little brighter. Less worried, less tired, less concerned about anything bad, so far this night was possibly the greatest, the peculiar child had ever had. Myshi wished she'd saved some of her snacks, but a little hunger would not hold her back. She smiled and studied the marvellous sight, of the unexplored world in the unexplored night. Countless trees which might well contain, more marvellous creatures with marvellous names. She'd never imagined such magical places, growing up surrounded by green clock towers, as she had discovered whilst exploring the night, for only a small number of hours. The grass was soft beneath her feet, the twilight breeze hummed a happy tune, Myshi wondered when it would be time to go home, and hoped it would not be too soon.

8

Across the sky a shadow moved, like an endless curtain being drawn, where there had been stars and blue, a black and yellow swarm. It seemed the swarm would grow forever, until all that could be seen, was an endless ocean in the sky, made up of buzzy bees. They were bees! They were bees! Millions of bees! The buzzy bees from the tales. Myshi realised and her eyes grew wide, and her skin seemed increasingly pale. As well as the terror, aroused by the swarm's unimaginable number, the really unsettling thing was the noise, crazier and louder than thunder.

The sound rose and fell, the bees numbers swelled, the swarm seemed to be out of control. Myshi Moo thought the monstrous bees, could eat a child in one go! Myshi Moo wondered where she could hide, from the incoming yellow and black buzzing tide, she couldn't see a hiding place, as the bees flew into every space. They covered the sky, they covered the moon, Myshi Moo felt dreadfully doomed. The world seemed to shrink and tighten around her, there was no light, only bees did surround her.

She felt the bees buzz around her legs, between her fingers, and on top of her head. Poor little Myshi wanted to scream, but thought the bees would fly into her throat, their furry bodies crawled all over her skin, and then, Myshi Moo started to float. She stayed perfectly still, only moving her eyes, somehow, so far, Myshi Moo had survived. She'd been sure she'd be killed by a million stings, but so far they hadn't done any such thing. They'd certainly terrified Myshi Moo, she'd never been so afraid in her life, but if she ignored the deafening buzz, floating on bees actually felt quite nice. Now as she floated the ceiling of bees, opened up so Myshi could see, above her once more was the moon up high, and Myshi was less certain she'd die.

She seemed to be moving incredibly fast, the stars and the clouds in the sky flew past, Myshi wondered how far she had gone, as she zoomed over the trees and the rocks, the bees wrapped around her and kept Myshi warm, and she wondered where they would stop.

Myshi could still hear the once awful hum, of the gargantuan buzzing cloud, but she didn't mind, she was having fun, and the buzzing no longer seemed loud. It was actually quite nice, somewhat musical, and it helped Myshi Moo to feel calm, and it was obvious to Myshi as she floated along, that the bees would do her no harm.

Like a ship on an ocean Myshi had covered, what seemed like hundreds of miles at least, but the path she had taken could not be discovered, it was only known by the bees. As well as the route something else was unknown, and that was her destination, for the place to which the bees had flown, was a land of isolation. An empty place where even the wind, felt alone and without a friend, and all day and night it would sadly sing, and wish the loneliness would end. It was a land without houses, or creatures or people, not a school in sight, not even a steeple. No sign of a park or a single toy store, a land like nothing you've seen before.

With a mellowing buzz the bees descended, and Myshi realised her flight had ended, as they placed her gently onto the floor, then quickly departed till their buzz was no more.

The cloud of bees was soon out of sight, and Myshi began to feel daunted, for nowhere else she'd been that night, had felt so definitely haunted. There was not a single blade of grass, not even a weed could take hold, she'd never heard of such an unsettling place, in all the tales she'd been told.

The breeze whistled past her tickling her ears, and Myshi heard herself say "well that was quite fun, and this wind is quite funny, it seems to be blowing both ways." Far off in the distance, Myshi could see, the wind picking up clouds of dust. It reached a point far away and made little tornadoes, then straight back towards her it rushed. Before the tornadoes, got anywhere near, they appeared to sink, and then disappear. The voices that sang, the wind's lonely song, become high pitched and frantic, then things really went wrong.

From far in the distance there came a terrible noise, like the sound of monster being woken, and it was a monster who definitely still wanted to sleep, not pleased that the peace had been broken. The sound was an awfully unpleasant moaning, with a power that made Myshi Moo want to run, but whatever misfortune was going to occur, had clearly already begun. It came from the place where Myshi had seen, the wind and the dust seem to fall into the ground, the earth beneath Myshi began to slope like a mountain, and nearly sent her tumbling down.

Wherever the bees had left Myshi Moo, was clearly a terrible place, and as she ran helplessly to somewhere unknown, she remembered the tales of the face. The groaning had morphed and become even more dreadful, it turned into hysterical laughter, and Myshi Moo screamed as she became quite certain, this would not end happily ever after.

9

Mr Moo was absorbed in deep introspection; his mind was pulling in different directions. One half said he must find Myshi or die, the other half didn't even want to try. His heart was all set, as was his soul, on finding his daughter, that was his goal. But as he doggedly continued into the night, something was telling him to give up the fight.

When he'd left the grass full of horrible eyes, he'd been utterly elated that he'd survived. He'd felt well on his way, after not being eaten, to finding his Myshi, sure he wouldn't be beaten. But that sense of certainty had morphed into doubt, and he began to regret, ever venturing out. Out into the darkness, the great unknowable unknown, what if he never found Myshi, what if she'd already gone home? What might lie ahead, Mr Moo speculated, he had not a clue, but felt very ill fated. What of the ghouls and the ghosts, and the things in the stories, all those things that were horrid, all those fates that were gory? Being eaten alive, or stung by the bees, or discovering the terrors, of those old trumpet trees. And what if he escaped, all of the foretold, there was still the ultimate horror, for him to behold. The hideous being, that had stalked him in dreams, and turned years of childish slumber, into nightmares and screams.

Since he'd had Myshi Moo, he'd not had such dreams, now she was missing, what did that mean? Would he no longer have peace, was he no longer safe, was he destined to face, the frightening face?

Something moved in the distance, Mr Moo turned his head, away from endless thoughts and what ifs, back to the real world instead. Against an inky twilight, on the vast empty plain, there was something enormous, towards him it came. Its shape was uncertain, it seemed to expand, as it rapidly advanced, to where he did stand. Mr Moo stood aghast, frozen with terror, it seemed his adventure had been a terrible error. He thought about running back to the grass, but it was clearly no good, the thing was too fast. All of the scenarios, in Mr Moo's head, ended up the same way, with Mr Moo dead. He fell to his knees, and screamed at the sky, he feared he had failed, and he feared he would die.

For it seemed as if doom had turned into a thing, an inescapable fate, now closing in. It turned the night sky into a dark murky mire, Mr Moo felt certain he was about to expire. The dark shadow fell like an endless black cloth, it wrapped all around him and raised him aloft. Its terrible din extinguished his voice, and aware of his capture, the frightening face did rejoice.

Deep in the hole, in the far away place, the night was being watched by the frightening face. In his eerie abode, he looked into the night, omniscient being, all things in his sight. He had watched Myshi Moo, both angered and awed, no human had come, this far before. The grass and the trees, and the things in between, could not stop this young girl, fearless she seemed. And the frightening face, almost cracked a strange smile, he knew he'd meet the strange girl in a while. Inevitable it was, that she would arrive, he clapped his hands, and hissed "She'll be here in five!" He laughed a troubling laugh, it gurgled and shrieked, his icy breath hissed and his skinny limbs creaked. He lit a small fire, with the spark from a stone, and his shadow danced madly, on the walls of his home. His blue eyes became wider, so he looked undeniably mad, expecting the first visitor, he'd ever had.

10

Myshi Moo looked down at her shoes, she knew there was no going back, too late to wonder what to do, the land was turning black. Not the blackness of the night, where light comes gently from the moon, but a shadow swallowing the earth, and bringing with it dreadful gloom. Around her still, there was some light, like a protective shell. Within persisted strands of light, whilst all around her darkness fell. It came not only from above, but crept in from all around, the darkness was unstoppable, annihilating all it found. It was as if the world was paper, upon which ink had been spilled, and if the ink reached Myshi, Myshi knew she would be killed.

So she focused on her feet, just her shoes upon the ground, trying not to think about, the terror all around. Light remained within the shell, the fragile walls kept darkness out, and hope remained in Myshi's heart, but in her head was fear and doubt. On the ground in front of her, the most peculiar thing, a narrowing path of pale blue light, that grew as skinny as a string. Off into the distance, the path of light carried on, but the shadow was getting closer, and all the light would soon be gone. Myshi's heartbeat was rapid, tears began to fill her eyes, she ran as quickly as she could, Myshi didn't want to die.

The darkness seemed to sense her fear, as she ran it screamed, Myshi cried but did not stop, for there was something she had seen. There seemed to be a tiny sunset, the final source of light, and she was sure if she could reach it, she would escape the endless night. Before the darkness extinguished, the light ahead and on the floor, before she became part of the shadow, and disappeared forever more. Through her sobs and frightened screams, Myshi heard a frightening voice, "Run faster girl! Run to me! You do not have a choice!"

She willed her tired legs to run, as fast as they would go, she saw the light ahead was coming, from some kind of hole. A glowing crater in the earth, at least twenty Myshi's wide, the final light and frightening voice, emanated from inside. "You must outrun the shadow, you must outrun the dark, if the darkness touches you, it will stop the beating of your heart!" Myshi's lungs felt like they'd burst, her hand covered her face, she leapt into the glowing pit, towards the undiscovered place.

Now all around was bright white light, Myshi kept on falling, booming laughter now replaced, the voice that had been calling. The white hole seemed to have no end, it was incomparably deep, endless descent began to send, Myshi Moo to sleep.

The girl who'd never ever slept, who every night a vigil kept, the child who'd never had to rise, now struggled to open her hazel eyes. No longer could she hear the laughter, as she fell towards some ever after, as the hole kept pulling Myshi under, it seemed that Myshi Moo might slumber. And as she tumbled through the never, Myshi's eyelids came together, and bit by bit her eyelids closed, and Myshi Moo appeared to dose. Her hair trailed up as she descended, into the pit that never ended, body limp and face relaxed, then all at once her world turned black.

11

When time uncounted had elapsed, the visitor did stir, and other than the trees perhaps, no one else knew where they were. For the visitor was not alone, but certainly she was the first, except the host to fall into, this place that you might think was cursed. This place where nobody ever came, where every moment was the same, where only a bee heard the unhinged screams, of the boy who could be seen in dreams. The boy was sitting close to Myshi, but could not easily be seen, he wondered why although he tried, he could not access Myshi's dreams.

His pale blue eyes in orbs of white, were eagerly inspecting, the girl he'd watched on her night time adventure, the girl he'd been expecting. The first visitor he'd ever had, since becoming the frightening face, except for a particular bee, no one had ever been to his place.

He'd been alone, since he'd left his home, in a place he'd never forgotten, for it was where he'd lost his parents, all his memories were rotten.

So much had been wrong, so little had been right, but in this cave one fateful night, the boy had found a means to pay back, all of the insults and all of the slights. In every place that he'd ever been, the children had been exceptionally mean. They'd call him 'Spooky' and 'Ghost boy', made fun of his pale white skin, the boys and the girls would play their games, but never let him join in.

His only constant company, was a kindly bumble bee. The bee brought him honey and used its wings to buzz songs, the bee thought he'd never done anything wrong. The bee was kind, and the bee was wise, and the bee wished the boy, would soon realise, that the world is not fair, and the world does not care, and if you're a little bit different, it's hard out there. So one night the bee, whose name was Stripy, had buzzed to the boy, "come follow me." And out into the night, whilst everyone slept, the bee had gone buzzing, and the little boy crept.

12

New shadows slid on sunny streets, behind one closed door there was defeat, the sun had come back to the green clock tower town, and Myshi Moo had not been found. In the East the sun had risen, another day the land was given, golden sunshine warmed the streets, but still two hearts did sadly beat. Birdsong rose as the people yawned, but two sad souls were all forlorn.

Between two worlds there was a chasm, that only one before had crossed, the path between them never fathomed, and now another had been lost. This other world a lonely place, where Frightening Face had lived alone, now that same sadness filled the void, which had been Myshi's home. Just as it had so long ago, filled another place, where once there lived that little boy, who had become the face. Out of a house where nobody went, where many lonely days he'd spent. With nobody to call a friend, he'd quietly hoped the hurt would end. The hurt caused by being on his own, in a village where kindness had rarely been shown. Not to the boy whose parents had died, the unusual boy with sad blue eyes, the boy who no one understood, the boy who'd been ostracised.

How long ago, the boy did not know, for he had no clocks, no fast or slow. In his lair, he did not care, he played his game, of spreading fear. Inside the cave, the bee had found, he found a crystal on the ground, unlike anything he'd found before, and after that, he'd found some more. And can you guess what he discovered, about that crystal and the others? With the crystals, was a way, to enter minds as they lay sleeping, for he could go into their rooms, then in their heads he could go creeping. And should we really be surprised, to learn the little boy who tried, to be friends with the other children, now chose to leave them terrified?

The boy had cried so many years, and those children had laughed at his tears, and now he filled his nights with fun, by filling theirs with fear. Revenge! Revenge! Sweet in the end! With all the terror he created, the little boy believed he could mend. The boy who lived in misery, was happy now that he could be, inside the dreams of enemies, spreading fear like a disease.

In his isolated home, the second one that he had known, for the first time in his lonely life, he was no longer on his own. He had his victims in their beds, and everyday he'd have his bread, in his cave with Stripy the bee, who brought him bread and fresh honey. As they ate, he'd laugh and sing, about scaring bullies and such things, the boy who'd been ostracised, his magic crystals by his side. He had power, he had fun, he wasn't the tormented one. And he was sure when they awoke, in the town the children spoke, about the boy who'd been ignored, and now in nightmares they all saw. He'd creep up on them pulling faces, or take their dreams to awful places, he'd plant horror in their heads, and sometimes they would wet their beds.

At that moment he wasn't sure, what he should do with

what he saw, the girl who lay upon his floor, who he'd never seen in dreams before. For some time now he'd watched her travel, for the crystals could unravel, all that happened in the night, beyond just dreams they gave him sight. The crystals opened up the darkness, they showed him everything, and for some time he'd watch this stranger, for some time he'd been wondering. Now she lay some feet away, and the boy did not know what to say. He held the crystals in his hand, he simply didn't understand. As she lay sleeping, somehow keeping, him from entering her dreams, the blue-eyed boy could not be certain, what this anomaly could mean. How could it be, he could not see, inside her head he could not tread? He placed his palms upon her skull, that's how he got inside, but dreams seemed to be void and null, no matter what he tried.

Was she asleep, did she pretend, what could this visitor portend?

13

Of darkness little now remained, in the world Myshi had left, sat silently with teary eyes, her parents were bereft. Her mother and her father too, they had both made up their minds, if Myshi Moo wasn't home for tea, they would leave the world behind. Mrs Moo at first had pleaded, when Mr Moo returned, Myshi Moo was all she needed, but then she had discerned. The look upon her husband's face, the trembling in his gait, the knowledge of what he had seen, resigned them to their fate. He'd told her all about the night, the places he had been, about the horror of it all, and all the things he'd seen. Sat around the table as the hours slowly slipped away, all the Moos could hope for, was tea later that day. For Myshi Moo had written, and asked them not to worry, she said that she'd be back for tea, they wished tea time would hurry.

 Sadness had created haste, and once their minds were made, they felt they had no time to waste, the table had been laid. A full six hours before time, a plethora of treats prepared, they sat waiting for their child, silent as the hour neared. Four pm, time for tea, they couldn't wait to see Myshi. They knew that she would be on time, it was part of her design, their perfect child always true, to the things she said she'd do.

 On the other side of that decision, the expectation of precision, was another certainty, there was no such thing as a late Myshi. Without speaking her parents knew, if just one minute, and at most two, elapsed beyond the chime of four, and Myshi wasn't at the door, it must mean she would never be, and they'd have lost their progeny. The light would go out in their world, as had gone their little girl.

"What if she doesn't…" said Mr Moo.

"Then we know what we must do." Mrs Moo looked straight ahead, considering what she had said. A thought before unthinkable, had now become their resolution, but after they had planned it all, they could not find an elocution. The only sound was of their breath, slow and deep and steady, Mrs Moo said, "It's only death, shall I get it ready?"

"It's done" came Mr Moo's reply, he rose and walked out of the room, returning with a little bottle, and two silver spoons. He placed the spoons down on the table, next to the chocolate and the treats, before putting on his glasses, and returning to his seat.

Holding hands with Mrs Moo, the other slipped into his pocket, and from there his shaking hand produced, a neatly folded docket. Placed down upon the tabletop, it showed ingredients and instructions, of the bottle that was tidily labelled, 'Slow Sleepy destruction.' They both read all the lines again, as they had several times before, hoping to discard the poison, when Myshi Moo knocked on the door. Hoping they would be okay, when the clock struck four.

14

Across the chasm, down the hole, beyond the trumpet trees, there was a girl, and a boy, and a magic bee. As the girl lay silently, the boy and bee had waited, now out of patience they'd become, perplexed and agitated. Agitation of the buzzing kind, it was the boy who felt perplexed, for this visitor had no signs of dreaming, that his crystals could detect. Then in a voice heard ever so rarely, a voice not heard by anyone nearly, a voice that made the bumblebee shake, the frightening face said softly and clearly, "I wish she was awake."

A declaration of this kind, almost cost the bee her mind. Coming from the frightening face, the words seemed utterly out of place. The frightening face who had refused for years and years on end, to go back to the distant town, where he swore he had no friends. The town from which the boy had come, where the boy had said he knew no one. No one that he could call a friend, no one who understood, he'd tried his hardest to fit in, but trying did no good.

The children taunted "Look at you! Why are your eyes so big and blue, and why do you wear those funny clothes, why do you speak the way you do?" The frightening face had been called names, he'd been left out of all the playground games, not because of anything, except that he was not the same. By the time the boy was eight, he was angry and consumed by hate, his parents were both hit by lightning, and he was left alone. No one came to comfort him, he buried his parents all alone, no one came to the funeral, and he never went back home.

The little bee sat on a rock, intrigued and yet completely shocked, for what the bee sat there observing, was fascinating and unnerving. For aeons she had only seen, her companion act wild and mean, taking undisguised delight, in frightening everyone at night. All his habits demonstrated, that he passionately hated, with every ounce of energy, those he considered enemies. That included everyone, all the daughters and the sons, for everyone had seemed malicious, and that had made him rather vicious.

Since he had learned the crystal's power, each night he stalked the green clock towers, filling sleeping heads with terrors, to pay back their ancestors' errors. Erroneously they'd kept taunting, the boy who wasn't quite the same, and now the boy had great fun haunting, and Frightening Face became his name. How fitting it had always been, for the face that made the children scream, but the boy now sitting by the bee, seemed to have woken from a dream. There was no mischief in his face, of wickedness there was no trace, he just sat quietly contemplating, a curious boy quietly waiting. The boy who'd been so long a ghoul, didn't seem ghoulish at all, he was not being the frightening face, but a curious boy in a curious place.

The bee wondered what would occur, as they both sat watching her, the first visitor they'd ever had, and then, the visitor began to stir. The boy and bee were both transfixed, as the little girls eyelids twitched, she stretched her limbs a little while, and then the visitor seemed to smile. All the time her eyes stayed closed, and she reached up and scratched her nose. The visitor took a hungry breath, filling her nostrils and her chest. She sat up and sighed, then quietly said, "Oh, where am I?"

The boy and bee both held their breath, as if to breathe would bring them death, for so long they'd been on their own, and visitors had been unknown. Accustomed to themselves they'd grown, how to host guests, they'd not been shown.

Myshi was not really sure, how'd she'd arrived upon the floor, she remembered following the light, and the growing darkness of the night. She remembered landing with a thump, she rubbed her heard and found a bump. Myshi thought and Myshi mused, how she had come to be quiet bruised, and for her current situation, she sought an explanation. The answer came in little time, a memory in her marvellous mind, Myshi knew she'd figured it out, she'd not been sleeping, she'd been knocked out! Perhaps even before she'd landed, her faculties had been disbanded, her body and brain had separated, maybe she'd been asphyxiated. The lump reminded Myshi Moo, of something she had once been told, regarding subtle differences, between being asleep and being out cold. The second of those situations, could be caused by strangulation, or some other thing that limited, the oxygen inside one's head. Certainly the things she'd seen, could have given her a shock, and if not the places that she'd been, maybe landing on solid rock!

All of it was useless musing, as far as Myshi was concerned, now that she'd regained her senses, there were things for her to learn. Myshi Moo was satisfied, there was no mystery to think about, it didn't take long to decide, she'd not been sleeping, she'd been knocked out. She was simply glad she'd woken, and grateful that no bones were broken. She blinked her eyes to check her vision, before she made any decisions, she felt that it would be remiss, not to check for damaged wrists, or any formerly unseen bumps, and cuts or strains, any bleeding, any pain, any damage to her brain. Satisfied with her condition, sound of body and cognition, Myshi Moo felt rather good, unaware of what behind her stood.

The audience behind her back, didn't know how to react, should they see if she was friendly, or stage a pre-emptive attack? If not to strike, then what to do? Neither moved as neither knew. Should they treat her as a welcome guest, or an intruder and a pest? Should they hide before she saw them, they had no idea what would be best. Dumbfounded they made not a sound, as they waited for her to turn around. The silent hosts began to tremble, neither sure what to expect, then Myshi turned to face them both, they all wondered what would happen next.

Myshi took a step forward, but not a word was spoken, the boy in kind stepped forward too, the ice yet to be broken. Myshi felt intimidated, inside the cave with this stranger, in someone else's territory, she knew there could be danger. She tried to put out of her mind, anything she feared, but could not ignore the fact this boy, looked particularly weird. In the luminescent cave, his skin was like porcelain, the whitest thing shed ever seen, and he was really much too thin. His eyes were large and lonely looking, with an unfamiliar hue, it was the first time Myshi Moo had seen, eyes of such deep blue. Myshi tried a little smile, but her face seemed set like clay, she scrambled for a greeting, but found no words to say. A glint of light caught her attention, at the end of his skinny arms, he held a long sharp crystal, did he mean her harm? Was this how her life would end, was she going to be slaughtered, butchered with a crystal dagger, the Moo's one and only daughter?

As if the boy had read her mind, he raised the dagger above his head, Myshi was ready to fight for her life, but really wished she'd stayed in bed. Myshi raised her little hands, was this the final curtain? She didn't know the boy as well, was feeling very uncertain. As we tend to do when we're unsure, the boy did as he'd done before, he pulled the most horrific face, and let out a diabolical roar.

It was a practised mechanism, designed to cause great fear, the most terrifying act he had, it had worked for years and years. His roar grew even more menacing, he waved his arms around, but something strange was happening, he heard a long- forgotten sound. At first he tried to drown it out, but it could not be denied, a sound that made him want to run, and find a place to hide. He redoubled his efforts, to be most horrifying, but he was hurt by what he heard, there was no point in trying. The roar became a whisper, the grimace disappeared, his arms dropped to his sides, his cheeks glistened with tears.

"Stop it!" he pleaded, his hands covered his ears, the pale boy began to sob, then ran away and disappeared. No longer frightened, Myshi felt bad, was it her reaction, that had made him so sad? When he'd contorted his face, and started to roar, it was unlike anything, she'd witnessed before. It was so unexpected, it was so hilarious, but now all at once, things all seemed so serious. The bee hovered nearby, wobbling sadly, the last few minutes, had gone quite badly.

Myshi had laughed, at what she had seen, and reminded the boy of who he had been. The ridiculed child, shunned by his peers, their tormenting laughter, had burned his ears. The sad little outcast, who'd been ostracised, the one who'd been ignored, when his parents died. The boy who had learned, that children were cruel, had dared to hope for a friend, and felt like a fool.

Myshi looked guiltily at the ground, and then looked back at the bee, she shuffled her embarrassed feet, and said, "Why did he run away from me?" The bee hovered over, it flew close to her ear, and then the tiniest voice, said, "It's okay my dear." Then the bee flew away, buzzing solemnly, Myshi just heard it say, "Come on, follow me. I've never seen him so upset, not since he first arrived, for many days and many nights, all he did was cry. I brought him here to let him hide, I thought he might die of sorrow, every night I buzzed him to sleep, and said you'll feel better tomorrow.

Here he stayed, and I stayed close, after some time, he was far less morose. When I gave him bread and fresh honey, he eventually managed to smile, I thought he'd eat a little and leave, but he's been here for a while."

Myshi followed close behind, listening to the bee, joining dots inside her mind, and marvelling at the scenery. She was by now quite sure she'd found, the undiscovered place, and judging by what she had seen, the boy must be the frightening face. By turns the cave was bright and dark, with a marvellous plafond, of rock and crystal stalactites, and occasional sparkling ponds. In a narrowing unlit passage, where the ceiling was much lower, the bee stopped talking altogether, and began to fly much slower. Then it turned back to Myshi, and led her to a little boulder, upon the boulder Myshi sat, the bee sat on her shoulder. For some time they did not move, Myshi wondered why, then the bee said "I have to go but I'll be back, if you promise you won't cry." And just like that, off it flew, quickly flying out of view, leaving Myshi on the boulder, wondering what to do. Where was the bee, where was the boy, the 'frightening face' as he was known, why had she laughed and made him cry, and why had she been left alone?

15

All of the clocks in the town with green towers, showed five minutes until the sixteenth hour, since the clocks struck twelve the night before, meaning it was five to four. On tables in houses on all of the streets, families were getting ready to eat, arranging the cutlery and setting the plates, though some did it earlier and some would be late. In one house the minutes ticked slower it seemed, with each tick of the clock like the sound of a gun, around a table displaying chocolate treats, the Moos were praying their daughter would come. They'd fretted and fidgeted, but now all they could do, was sit and wait, for their Myshi Moo. With each drawing of breath, with each creeping second, salvation or death, ceaselessly beckoned.

They'd made the tea, they'd weighed their options, prepared the table, and the concoction. As the hour, had grown close, they'd both measured, and poured their dose. Between their cups of toxic brew, was the note from Myshi Moo. If the words, became untrue, they knew exactly what to do. If she was not there by five past four, they would go to sleep, forever more.

The clock struck four, the clock towers chimed, they watched their door, it was tea time. Two minutes passed, still no sound, a silent tear, splashed on the ground. No one came, no one knocked, the Moo's both wished, the clocks would stop. But time would not wait, for the sake of the

Moo's, by four o' eight, there was nothing to lose.

Mr Moo squeezed Mrs Moo's hand, "What do we do?"

"We do as we planned."

He took the hand- written note, and pressed it to his face, he turned to his wife, and they gently embraced. They wiped each other's tears, and nodded their heads, they both drank the poison, and headed to bed. They lay side by side, "I love you" they said. Six hours later, they'd both be dead.

16

Myshi was hungry, she had nothing to eat, she was tired of waiting, she got to her feet. The bee had not returned, not yet anyway, there was no one to speak to, and nothing to play. *How lonely* thought Myshi, *it must be in this place,* and she found herself thinking, about Frightening Face. *Did he have any parents, siblings or friends, was he really so frightening, or was it pretend?* The first time she'd seen him, he was certainly no beast, until he began roaring, and pulling faces at least. But any child, could do that if they tried, what troubled Myshi, was that he had cried.

Now she was sat, with no plan in her mind, and it seemed the bee, had gone and left her behind. Myshi started speculating, her predicament being rather frustrating, and she'd had enough of waiting, the bee had said it would be back. Considering her situation, with no idea of her location, she felt she had to find the boy, but she might get lost without a map. She'd come so far since leaving home, she'd learnt a lot she hadn't known, she had no clue how long she'd been gone, but knew that she would have to go back. She'd left well aware, that her parents would worry, like everyone else they were scared of the night, they believed the night was full of monsters, and if she didn't get back, they'd believe they were right!

With an impatient growl, she jumped off of the rock, and decided it was time to explore, and before very long something caught her attention, something she hadn't noticed before. Maybe ten metres from where she'd been sitting, was a turning off to the right, and when Myshi found it entirely by chance, she saw an encouraging sight. At the end of the passageway, to which she had come, Myshi saw light, suggesting the sun. Could it be a way out of the cave, had the night been replaced by the day? Towards the source of the illumination, she hastily made her way.

Just beyond the corridor, there was something else that Myshi saw, it stopped little Myshi in her tracks, he was sitting on the floor. The frightening face, the boy who'd cried, was sitting, crystals by his side. He had not seen Myshi, her distance she kept, sat in the shadows, he quietly wept. Myshi watched with growing concern, then came a soft buzzing, the bee had returned. They both watched and listened silently; the bee and Myshi Moo, the boy wept inconsolably, they wondered what to do.

Myshi entered the vast stony chamber, like an uninvited stranger, intruding on the frightening face, trespassing in his private place. The bee followed closely behind her, it kept on buzzing to remind her, that while she seemed to be alone, she was not really on her own. Approaching the boy took wilful persistence; nervously she closed the distance, driven on by her own conscience, and the buzzing bee's insistence. A few feet away from where he was sat, Myshi discontinued walking, it was close enough and she was sure, that the boy would hear her talking. But Myshi did not say a thing, she wanted him to speak, she stood there nervous and wondering, feeling unusually meek. Myshi felt stuck, she could not budge, Stripy the bee gave her a nudge. The boy still paid them no attention, wallowing in his misery, not fully convinced by her own intention, she moved close enough for him to see. Though his head was in his hands, she'd be in his field of sight, unless of course whilst he was weeping, the boy kept both of his eyes shut tight. She wanted to apologise, she wanted to understand, she wanted to know about the boy, she slowly extended her hand.

His head stayed down and the tears kept flowing, whether or not he knew she was there, Myshi Moo had no way of knowing, maybe he knew but did not care. She felt so small in the cavern so spacious, she mustered her courage, but remained trepidatious. She managed a "please…" only one word, and there was no doubt at all that her "please" had been heard.

The boy leapt up, he lashed at the air, as if fighting a beast that was not really there, he howled like an animal, he hissed and he spat, Stripy and Myshi were taken aback.

"I hate you," he screamed, "you're just like them! And when I first saw you I thought we'd be friends!" Now things were really deteriorating, Myshi had been misunderstood, so Myshi Moo decided to do, what any intelligent person should. She folder her arms whilst the boy threw his fit, and eventually he quietened down a bit. Myshi Moo simply would not engage, he could not keep up his fit of rage. He jumped and stomped upon the floor, less frequently he tried to roar, but with less conviction than before, whatever he did, he was ignored.

At length his energy abated, as Myshi had anticipated, she knew that he would soon give in, that was when she would begin. Silence replaced the erstwhile howling, his shoulders slumped, there was no more scowling, exhausted and defeated too, he manage to whisper one more "I hate you."

The boy sat down and hugged his knees, holding his arms with trembling hands, he was joined by his friend the buzzing bee, it was just as Myshi Moo had planned. She examined at length the sorry sight, framed by the pale beams of light, the boy and the bee looking sad and alone, in the endless cave that was their home.

"I'm sorry" started Myshi Moo, "I'm sorry that I laughed at you, but the way you acted when we met, it's not really what people do. I don't think that I understood, but the face you pulled was very good!"

She looked directly at the boy, the bee was sitting on his head, so far the boy had not reacted, to anything that Myshi had said.

"Well, your behaviour, I was saying, I think I must have been confused. I wasn't sure if you were playing, but admit I was amused. My laugh was not inspired by cruelty, your interpretation there was faulty. I'm just used to most first meetings, starting with a simple greeting; like "hi" you know, or just "hello." With friends you might say "how have you been" but no one starts with a mighty scream! That's what took me by surprise, the way you screamed and moved your eyes! When you made that frightening face, it made me laugh, in any case, I did not want to make you cry, I'd like to have another try."

The boy looked up with eyes of blue, she quietly said, "I'm Myshi Moo."

The boy stood up, his features strained, he timidly nodded his head, he tried to smile, but looked quite strange, as if his smile was dead. As if his cheeks, had drooped too long, and could not be lifted up, as if his lips would no longer bend, as if his face was stuck. Stuck in expressions of misery, of anger and dejection. All of the faces one might wear, if they only knew rejection. Then with a voice that was quiet and calm, and with a nervously held out palm, making progress with his smile, he said, "Sorry, it's been a while."

With those words, the bee took flight, buzzing wildly with delight. It seemed a spell had just been broken, with those words the boy had spoken. The bee flew in loops and figures of eight, there was clearly cause to celebrate. Stripy wanted to hear whatever was said, but knew it was time to fetch honey and bread.

"We've never had a visitor. Where do I begin? It's a shock to meet you Myshi Moo. By the way, my name is Finn."

"Hello Finn, how do you do? Who else lives in this cave with you?"

"There's no one else, just me and the bee, now you're here as well, that makes three."

Myshi Moo considered the boy, he looked so harmless standing there, but she was sure he was the frightening face, she wondered if he was aware. She'd never dreamt, so had no proof, but everyone else, called it the truth. Myshi's friends and parents too, and everybody else they knew, had seen him when their eyes were closed, and been terrified as they dosed, and told each other when they arose, about the terrible frightening face.

As Myshi had been following the light, a little earlier that night, the voice she'd heard gave her a fright, calling her to the cave. But now she stood there with a stranger, a little boy called Finn, there was nothing there suggesting danger, except perhaps for the hole they were in. She worried that she might not get home, she'd had quite enough adventure, her parents were going to be terribly cross, and stress could increase their chance of dementia.

Myshi's mind accelerated, she needed more information, she knew her best source of new data, was going to be conversation.

"Finn. That's a nice name. I like this place. Have you ever heard of the frightening…?"

Myshi did not say the name and Finn would not have heard, for the bee had noisily returned, drowning out her words. Somehow balanced on its back, was a well-proportioned dome, it was made up of brown and golden hues, largely bread and honeycomb. Myshi suddenly felt the pain, of hunger long ignored, she'd barely eaten anything, since the day before. She wondered what the time must be, how long since she left home, she thought that if she didn't eat soon, she might become just a bag of bones.

The bee landed on a rock near Finn, invisible beneath the dome, "Share the food" the bee called out, "Myshi make yourself at home!"

Finn plunged a hand into the pile, it was covered with honey up to the wrist, then he shoved it into his mouth and sucked, the bee said, "Myshi, eat, I insist." Finn continued with disregard, his arms were shiny with honey and spit, Myshi took honeycomb from the dome, before Finn could put his hands on it. Seeming to sense Myshi's alarm, at the way her new acquaintance ate, the bee dropped honey and bread at Finn's feet, then gave Myshi what was left on the plate. It sympathised with Myshi Moo, shaking its furry little head, Myshi wanted to cover her ears, as Finn noisily gobbled a piece of bread. He sucked his hands and licked his fingers, with noisy mastication; Myshi quietly ate and watched, with secretly disgusted fascination.

    She wondered what had made him so, could it be he'd never been shown, any manners or etiquette, how long had this cave been his home? As she watched her feral host, she began imagining his past, but she knew it was foolish to assume, there were questions she had to ask. With her best inquisitive tone in mind, determined not to sound rude, Myshi got ready to start talking, as soon as he finished his food. He swallowed his final morsel, Myshi knew what she wanted to say, but before she could get his attention, Finn jumped up and ran away.

17

This was not good, Myshi was cross, if Finn would not talk, all might be lost. She sighed heavily, and called out his name, but there was only an echo, no reply came. All at once she was breathing much faster, what if her night, became a disaster? A sad misadventure, an errand for fools, the end of the girl, who ignored all the rules! A girl whose life would end underground, away from her family, a girl never found.

Myshi Moo panicked, she was not having fun, she began to regret, everything she had done. She wanted to quit, she didn't want to be brave, what Myshi Moo wanted, was to be saved. But who would save her, and save her from what, if Myshi did nothing, she'd die and she'd rot. Away in a cave, miles from home, where there might be beasts, to chew the flesh from her bones.

All of the years, of continuous waking, had made Myshi Moo, superb at debating. She had steadily acquired, vast cognitive wealth, which allowed Myshi Moo, to debate with herself. Whether her actions were judged as defective, was entirely contingent, upon her perspective. Any outcome, she could want or expect, must be brought about, by what she did next. She did not call him again, but instead started running, she didn't want Finn, to know she was coming. She'd concluded already, that he might be afraid, if he knew she was following, he could easily evade.

Her decision did not prove wrong, she was glad that she'd given chase, not far ahead she heard some kind of song, sung by the frightening face. The words were mixed in, with growls and shrieks, then Myshi saw him, neck deep in a creek. The water explained, some of what she had heard, the sounds of splashing and gurgling mixed in with the words. "You hurt me, you hate me, well I hate you too, and when you go to bed, I'll come after you. You cannot escape, you can't stay awake, as soon as you're under I'll give you a shake. Hahaaa! I wanted to play, you pushed me away, you thought I was gone, but you're going to pay. I hate you I hate you, nobody cares, I can't wait till bedtime, that's when I'll appear. Your parents are sleeping, my parents are dead, I'm coming for you, when you go to bed." Finn's tone did not match, the words in the song, it was rather jovial, Myshi nearly hummed along. Myshi approached, the edge of the creek, Finn did not see her, and she did not speak. He repeated the song, occasionally screaming, mocking the victims, who'd be lying there dreaming. He seemed entirely content, though he must have been freezing, when he got out of the water, he was shivering and wheezing. His skinny arms were crossed over, his skinny pale chest, his trousers were soaking, and so was his vest, despite his evident discomfort he did not seem distressed. He tiptoed and leapt, as if to keep himself limber, then from behind a large stalagmite, produced an armful of timber. He carried the load along the edge of the water, to a spot that was concaved and dark, from his soaking pocket he pulled a crystal, which he banged on the ground to make sparks. The sparks were large and incredibly bright, and in no time at all, the wood was alight.

Shadows danced upon the walls, beasts cast by the fire, Finn sat close to warm himself, and the flames grew hotter and higher. The wood cracked and popped, there was music and light, Finn looked at the fire and said, "Bring me the night."

The growing flames looked very inviting, Myshi crept closer as Finn kept reciting. "Bring me the night, bring me the night, I'll bring the terror, oh what a delight. Bring me the night, bring me the night, there are so many wrongs for me to put right. Put them to bed, they're all in error, put them to bed, I'll bring the terror." Then Finn said something entirely unexpected, for Myshi believed she had not been detected. "Why do you stand staring at the fire I've lit? Come closer now Myshi, come here and sit."

"Oh" spluttered Myshi, clearly surprised, "thank you" she said, averting her eyes.

She fumbled for words, but found nothing to say, Finn stared straight at her and said, "Are you okay?"

"I'm fine" she insisted, looking about, "this cave is so cosy."

"Would you like to get out?"

"Erm, yes, I mean no! Is that a suggestion?"

"You can stay if you want, it's only a question."

"Oh yes, well, not now! What am I talking about? So I'm not trapped, that's good, is there a way out?"

"Yes, leave if you please, do not feel compelled, but I'm not going back there, I hate the world."

Knowing that she could get out, gave Myshi great relief, but still she wondered what events, had formulated

Finn's beliefs. Why did he say the things he said, what went on inside his head? If she knew about his history, he might not be such a mystery.

"Finn," she said with trepidation, "I was hoping for an explanation; are the things you're saying true, did people do something bad to you?"

"I hate everyone I've ever met, except my mum and dad, apart from them all human beings, are evidently bad. Yes, they did bad things to me, so my parents relocated, but we do not look the same as them, so in each new place new foes awaited, each time we moved, we still were hated. So we stopped moving in the end, and then my parents died, and I had not a single friend, so I found a place to hide."

Myshi was saddened by Finn's revelation, her empathy was rather advanced, but she did not agree with his misanthropy, so she decided to take a chance. "Oh Finn, that's awful, I'm really sorry, some people are really cruel, but there are a lot of good people too, you can't simply hate them all.

"Look at me," she said confidently, "I am Myshi Moo. I'm a human but I've not been mean, do you hate me too?"

"I don't know you, we've just met, I haven't made my mind up yet."

"Well, I know me and lots of others, and there are lots of good people you can discover. I understand why you've retreated, but what if you're wrong about human beings? If you continue to hide then you've been defeated, there are good people out there that you're just not seeing."

"I'm not defeated, come and see, come closer Myshi, sit with me. Wait till you see, what I can do, I'm not a victim

Myshi Moo. In this cave, I don't need friends, from here I can exact my revenge."

"What do you mean, what do you do, exact revenge on who?"

"On everyone, no one escapes, but it's still too early, they're all awake. When night time comes, I'll let you see, I might let you join in with me."

Myshi Moo could not agree, though she really did want to see, what Finn was going on about, but by night time she'd have missed her tea.

Now Myshi wondered what to do, for her dilemmas numbered two, Myshi sensed the invitation, was indicative of a breakthrough. She must proceed with utmost caution, or see the scene deteriorate, reducing his friendliness a portion, and fanning his proclivity to hate.

Finn turned his gaze on Myshi Moo, his eyes were full of anticipation, Myshi wondered what to do, there was no easy extrication. The hand in which Finn held his crystal, was invitingly extended, Myshi stepped towards him, unsure what she intended.

"Take it Myshi, take the crystal" Finn eagerly advised, Myshi followed his instruction, as if she'd been hypnotised. She sat down and gazed into the fire, her face reflected its golden light, Myshi Moo began to whisper, "Bring me the night, bring me the night." Finn started rocking back and forth, happily nodding his head, he watched Myshi's every move, greatly amused by what she said.

"That's it!" he exclaimed, "Bring me the night!" let's practise a little, so you get it right." Though nothing had been explicitly stated, and there was no absolute way of knowing, Myshi Moo had a firm premonition, about where things were going.

Finn was giddy with childish delight, in the company of Myshi Moo, she hadn't made fun or pushed him away, like everyone else used to do. She'd not even mentioned that his skin was too pale, or asked why his eyes were blue. Finn took the crystal back from her, and said, "I'll show you what to do."

He brandished it now with both arms extended, the tip pointing back at his head, "You might have to use some imagination, this won't work properly until they're in bed." Finn's blue eyes narrowed in concentration, his breathing was loud and slow, "the first step is simply to see in your mind, the place you want to go."

The crystal began emitting a light, a glowing serpentine cloud, it worked its way along Finns arms, then wrapped his head like a shroud. The cloud was deep blue, streaked with red, it made Finns eyeballs roll back in his head. Between his eyelids, was pure ghastly white, Myshi wanted to scream, but was far too polite. Then Finn started chuckling, but his lips did not shift, apparently he was a ventriloquist. From the frightening face came a terrible sound, it was the voice that had called, Myshi Moo underground. The tone of the voice portended destruction, but it had merely relayed simple instructions.

"The crystal is magic, it opens the door, between where you are now, and where you've been before. At this moment I'm walking, the streets of my town, I'm invisible there, so I can wander around. Nothing can stop me, I can walk through the walls, and they're none the wiser, look at these fools!" The frightening face, still wrapped in strange light, was turning its head, left and right. "I hate these people, they're everywhere! As soon as they're sleeping, I'll give them a scare."

"How will you scare them, if they don't know you're there, do you slam doors and throw things, or make things disappear?"

"Not quite Myshi Moo, we've only begun, when these fools are asleep, we can really have fun." That didn't sound good, if she knew anything at all, she knew when people were sleeping, they became vul nerable. "Yes, when they're unconscious, tucked up in their beds, I can make them see me, just by touching their heads.

They'll see this terrible face, I'll become their nightmare, I'll scare everyone, then I'll disappear." The face turned to Myshi, with an evil smile, it said, "You have a go, they'll be awake for a while." With a horrible crack, it dropped its chin, its eyes rolled back, and the face became Finn.

Finn's transformation stunned Myshi Moo, as did his description of what the crystal could do.

"So this crystal is magic, and I can go anywhere?"

"Yes. Just concentrate, and imagine you're there."

"And I'll be invisible, unheard and unseen?"

"Yes you will, unless you enter a dream."

Those last words dispelled Myshi Moo's doubts, dreams were something she'd only daydreamed about. All of her life, she'd been kept out, of the world that Finn was talking about.

She took the crystal from Finn and shuffled about, she

made herself comfortable, then she stretched her arms out. She already knew where she wanted to go, she wanted to see what her parents were making, the magic crystal started to glow, Myshi' Moo's little arms started shaking. She saw a blue light, streaked with red, encircle her arms, then her neck and her head. The slithering vapour, had her mesmerised, and it turned to pure white, her big hazel eyes. For a split second, the world was black, then Myshi's chin dropped, and her neck went 'CRACK!'

18

Myshi could see now, Finn had told her the truth, she looked at her house, a magpie perched on the roof. The setting sun, made the sky blue and pink, Myshi Moo did not stop to think. She rushed to knock on her front door, but ended up in the corridor. She was shocked for a second, but then she recalled, she was invisible, and could walk through walls! It wasn't just walls, Finn had been talking about, clearly front doors, could not keep her out. She wanted to know, what else she could do, so she jumped on the floor, and she went through that too. Myshi giggled then gasped down in the basement, she'd landed on her feet, amazed by her power she still wanted to see, if her parents were making chocolate treats.

The basement light was not turned on, Myshi did not orient, in her dimly lit excitement, through the basement wall she went. From the greater darkness of the soil, she hurriedly returned, for all she'd found beyond that wall, was the smell of death, and bugs and worms. Back inside the basement, she placed her hands upon the wall, and felt her way to the wooden stairs, that led up to the hall.

It was only a matter of seconds, before her eyes adjusted, she could see but still she wondered, if her powers could be trusted. Holding the wooden handrail, she wondered what to do, would she ascend the creaky steps, or would she just fall through? The first step was solid, Myshi

Moo did not drop, as quick as she could, she rushed to the top. She ran straight through the door to where the family ate, the table was crowded with an assortment of plates.

Her parents had made, all of her favourite things, Myshi Moo couldn't wait for tea to begin. The house seemed too quiet, where could the Moo's be? Her stomach began rumbling, as she looked at her tea. There were chocolate rolls, there was chocolate cake, there was chocolate mousse with chocolate flakes. The sight of it all, made her mouth water, she felt like the world's luckiest daughter. All of the effort her parents had made, made Myshi feel guilty, she wished she had stayed. She'd never forget the adventure she'd had, but now all that she wanted was her mum and her dad.

She bit her lip and blinked her eyes, suddenly shaken by concern; she needed to get back to her home, but what if she couldn't return?

It was time to stop, she loosened her grip, on the magical crystal that she held, at the very same moment, from a room in her house, somebody suddenly yelled. "Why are they sleeping? It's not yet night. What's going on Myshi? This doesn't seem right."

Instinctively Myshi glanced at the clock, it was a quarter past six her heart nearly stopped. She ran to the voice, and what she saw there, was the closest she'd come to having nightmares. In her parents' bedroom, the air seemed much colder, her parents seemed to be sleeping, but they seemed many years older. The window was open, the curtains rhythmically billowed, their breath turned to steam, that rose from their pillows. The Moos faced each other, in a languid embrace, her mother's skin seemed too pale, there were blue veins on her face. The sight of her father, left her unable to speak, he was a husk of himself, weathered and weak. Like a wolf besides carrion, next to the bed, stood the frightening face, eyes rolled back in his head.

"Myshi" he cackled "shall we enter their dreams? We could both frighten them, and laugh at their screams!"

"No!" cried Myshi, "Why are they in bed? I'm late for my tea! Why do the look dead?"

Finn studied her parents, they looked awfully unwell "Don't worry" he scoffed "they're not dead, I can tell."

Myshi's adventure was no longer fun, she cried and she ran, what had she done? She ran back to the kitchen, with no idea what to do, and something unfamiliar, came into view. An unfamiliar glass bottle on the table top, something about it made Myshi Moo stop. The bottle was open, and almost drained, inside it a little liquid remained. Myshi moved closer and picked up the bottle, what she saw on the label sent her mind reeling full throttle. She'd learned about symbols in books she'd been shown, and the one on the bottle was a skull and cross bones. She knew what that meant, there was no use denying, her parents had been poisoned, they weren't sleeping, they were dying!

The glass bottle shattered on the kitchen floor. Myshi frantically ran through the bedroom door. "Do it!" she commanded. "Get into their heads!" Finn was clearly surprised. Myshi Moo jumped on the bed, she landed by her mother, and sat on her thighs, then placed the palms of her hands, over Mrs Moo's eyes.

Instantly Myshi became a fierce warrior. She was riding a butterfly in a phantasmagoria. The butterfly landed and said, "See you at the feast" then left Myshi on a carrot with her mother and a beast. Myshi was wearing her normal attire, along with the things a warrior requires. She had incredible strength, courage and speed, and a two headed axe that was warlike indeed. On top of the carrot on an orange dead end, her mother was trapped with no way to defend. The beast was stalking Mrs Moo, it's talons all extended, if Myshi didn't do something soon, her mother's life would be ended.

She ran to the beast and swung the axe. One cutting edge sunk into its back. Myshi pulled out the axe and swung it again, she split the beast's head, exposing its brain. Fatally wounded, but still not deceased, the beast advanced on her mother on whom it wanted to feast. It would tear off her limbs and bite off her head, it would eat all of her flesh and mop the blood up with bread. Mrs Moo screamed and squeezed her eyes shut, ready to accept her fate. But Myshi the warrior had not given up, she knew it was not too late. On her belt was a scabbard, as one might well expect, she was a warrior after all, she plunged the dagger into the beasts neck and that finally made the beast fall. It sprawled on the carrot bleeding and wailing, Myshi Moo felt she was prevailing. Her mother saw her, at first she rejoiced, but then Myshi sensed, great fear in her voice. She'd been saved from a monster by her warrior child but her voice betrayed terror and her eyes looked wild.

"Myshi! You saved me! But what's wrong with you? What's wrong with your eyes? Are you a beast too?"

Myshi recalled what had happened to Finn, she could try to explain but where would she begin? Her eyes were pure white, rolled back in her sockets, and she was covered in blood, it was in her hair and her pockets.

"It's okay Mummy, I've come to save you. I know I look scary, but I'm still Myshi Moo."

"My baby, my Myshi, have you really come home? I thought you were gone. And I was alone."

Without any warning, the scenery changed. Myshi was realising, dreams can be strange. They walked side by side, through flowers and trees. There was a sense of contentment, and finality. They were both wearing white, the sun was low in the West, Mrs Moo said, "Now you're home, I can rest." She sat down by a tree, her back to its trunk, she smiled softly, the sun had finally sunk.

In the sparkling twilight, Mrs Moo closed her eyes. Myshi screamed "Mummy! Wake up or you'll die!" Her mother was slipping into the eternal abyss. Myshi Moo panicked; she could not allow this. "Mummy come back, you must wake up, hurry! I'm sorry I'm late, but I'm coming home don't worry!" Myshi was failing but she had to keep trying. Her mother wasn't sleeping, she was actually dying. Her eyes would not open, Myshi lost hope. She called Mrs Moo, she could no longer cope. Despair spread through her, sadness tore her apart, the thought of losing her mummy, froze Myshi's heart. She placed her head on Mrs Moo's lap, her whole life had been ruined by her childish mishap. Words, choking and broken, interrupted her cries, "Mummy! I love you, please Mummy, don't die." The twilight had faded, Myshi Moo was forlorn, she was utterly helpless, she wished she'd never been born.

19

He was jolted awake, covered in sweat, he checked his surroundings, he must not forget, what he'd seen in his nightmare, what he'd been told, he grabbed his wife's arms, her body was cold. He shook her and struggled, to keep in his head, what the frightening face had said.

"Wake up! Wake up! We made a mistake. Myshi Moo's coming home, she's just running late."

Mr Moo's dream had been interrupted, by the frightening face who had clearly instructed, that he must wake up and wake his wife up too, he told him he'd seen his dear Myshi Moo. At first Mr Moo doubted the words he was hearing, but then the frightening face told him what Myshi was wearing. The boy in his nightmare then howled in his face, he sat on his chest and held him in place. It was years since he'd felt such desperate fear, the frightening face, put its lips to his ear.

"Helloooooooo" it growled, "listen to me, if you make me a promise, I'll let you be." Mr Moo tried to fight, but felt little and weak, the frightening face grabbed his face, so Mr Moo couldn't speak. "You should be grateful, I'm saving your life. Promise me you'll wake up, and you'll wake up your wife. Whatever happens, you must both stay awake, she will be home for her tea, make no mistake." Then the frightening face let out a deafening roar, Mr Moo was so shaken, he nearly fell on the floor. He set to rousing his wife, shouting and shaking, louder and faster, until he saw she was waking.

Mrs Moo was confused when she opened her eyes, she said "what are you doing? Aren't we meant to die?"

"No!" shouted her husband, "We must stay alive!"

Invisible Myshi, gave Finn a high five.

"But I dreamt about Myshi, we sat by a tree, I have to go back there, she's waiting for me."

"Myhsi's not there, don't you dare fall asleep! We have to get up, I have a promise to keep!"

"Hahaa!" exclaimed Finn, from the foot of the bed "we did it Myshi, your parents aren't dead!"

Myshi shrieked with joy, still unheard and unseen, she was possibly the happiest, she'd ever been.

Her parents had risen, they'd both come back from the brink, they both staggered towards, the kitchen sink, they'd related their dreams, and then both suggested, they should try to dilute what they had ingested. They hastily drank, large tumblers of water, both now convinced, they had not lost their daughter. They both read again, Myshi's hand written note, then refilled their tumblers, and poured the lot down their throats.

20

Back in the cave with their eyes back in place, Myshi Moo danced with the frightening face. Around the fire they merrily capered, singing a triumphant song, Myshi and Finn hand in hand, with Stripy the bee buzzing merrily along.

"*I saved* my mummy and my daddy *as well!*" an exuberant Myshi giddily yelled.

"Your parents drank poison,"
"They thought they'd lost me,"
"They thought you would never go home for tea."
"The crystals are magic!"
"Just like I said."
"*And now* my mummy and daddy aren't *dead!*"

Finn stopped dancing with Myshi Moo, his face became sullen and he quickly withdrew. He sat by the fire, biting his tongue, and Myshi regretted what she'd just sung. Though a small celebration was surely deserved, Myshi Moo knew she'd hit a raw nerve. Her features knotted in consternation, what a thoughtless thing she had said, the frightening face looked hurt and angry, she wished he was singing and dancing instead.

Just seconds before they'd been having a ball, but now the cave was no fun at all. The fire hissed and embers cracked, Myshi moved closer to where Finn had sat. Myshi's voice seemed stuck in her throat, Finn seemed to bristle as Myshi approached. She grasped at the words, but the words seemed afraid, she moved her lips, but no sound was made.

Finn spoke first, three words, then he paused, his words made it clear, just what had caused, the end of the song and the slaying of joy, with vitriol said the orphaned boy; "Good for you Myshi Moo, and good for all the others too. You'll never know the pain I feel, because my mum and dad were killed. Not by war, not by ill health, but by the very world itself.

I can't deny it Myshi Moo, my world seemed cold until I met you. You almost altered my conviction, about everyone's evil predilection. Myshi Moo you made me think, you really took me to the brink, you almost changed my old opinion, I considered leaving my dominion. But what you just said reminded me, it robbed me of your kind distraction, there's nothing in the world for me, the world outside holds no attraction."

Finns words left poor Myshi Moo, unsure of what she ought to do, she knew that she must get back home, but did not want Finn to be alone.

"Finn, I'm sorry, don't be upset, I didn't mean to make you sad, we've had so much fun, I won't forget, you know the world isn't really bad."

"It is! They are! Everyone! The whole world is malicious. I can't wait for the night to come, I'm going to be extra vicious!" I'll frighten every single child, I'll fill their heads with fear, and I'll feel happier and more avenged, with every child's scream I hear!"

The frightening face had grown incensed, the embodiment of hate, and Myshi Moo was getting cross, she was already much too late. But Myshi was wise beyond her age, so she was willing to wait, she could not allow indiscriminate rage, there was no good to be found in hate.

"Why are you so mean? What gives you the right, to ruin those dreams and spread terror each night?"

"How dare you question me!" roared Finn, "I'll fill your night with endless terror."

"Well you can't do that because I don't dream, so I think you'll find that you are in error."

Finn pulled an atrocious face and began a dreadful howling, but Myshi Moo seemed unaffected by his screaming and his scowling. "Finn, I'm not afraid of you. I know it's just an act. You're not some horrifying beast, you're just a frightened boy in fact. A little boy who thinks it's clever, to terrorise those poor children. It's dreadful that your parents died, but the children didn't kill them!"

An expression Myshi hadn't seen, now sat where Finn's rage had been, a bewildered face that made it seem, like he'd been shaken from a dream. He looked hurt and surprised as well as confused, he looked as if he'd been disabused, of some faulty belief he'd long clung to, he looked directly at Myshi Moo.

Finn looked lost, he felt displaced, a boy without a home, as if all his years had been a waste, and he faced a great unknown. He wondered if he'd been a fool, he felt ashamed and all alone, had he done nothing good at all, since he'd run away from home? The crystals lying by the fire, he'd thought were his salvation, had turned him into something dire, they'd been his damnation. What could he do? He had no friends, and if he left his hiding place, the children might all recognise him as the frightening face. What about the grownups, would they recall him too, and think he was a monster, what would the grownups do? Where could he go now he'd become, the nightmare child for everyone? The ghoul who stalked them when they slept, who felt avenged when children wept. For just a little while, the doom had disappeared, he'd been a normal boy, not someone alone and scared. For just a fleeting moment, Finn had made a friend, but the past had come back fast, and brought that to an end.

Finn had no choice he could not leave, he'd been foolish to believe, just because of Myshi Moo, that his dreams might all come true. Dreams that he had long denied, ever since his parents died, the dream of being a boy with friends, he'd be alone until the end. He'd stay inside the giant hole, where no one else would ever go, the dreadful lonely living space, where he'd remain the frightening face.

Myshi Moo was all but done, she'd come as far as she could come, she'd nearly made a brand- new friend, but all things must come to an end. She wished that she could prove him wrong, show him that he could belong, but all Finn seemed to know was pain, she was sure they'd never meet again.

"Finn" she said "I have to leave, I'm sorry that we don't agree, but what you think and what you do, are both entirely up to you."

She paused and hoped he'd say something, maybe he'd apologise, but all he did was stare at her, with distant sad blue eyes.

"The whole world isn't really cruel, but you won't believe a word I say, I really have to get back home, can you please show me the way?"

The bee had watched the conversation, hovering in isolation, it flew to Myshi Moo and said, "I'll arrange your transportation." Myshi turned to follow, the bee flew off into the hollow, of the narrow and shadowy tunnel she'd found, and Myshi knew she was homeward bound. She was relieved but also sad, as she started walking, she felt her lips forming a frown, and then Finn started talking.

"It's okay Myshi, you weren't cruel, in fact I think you're wonderful. Must you leave now, won't you stay? We could eat fresh honey, every day! We'll laugh and sing and dance and play. Please Myshi Moo, can't you stay?"

Myshi was happily astounded, the bee was joyously dumbfounded, at that moment deep within the cave, good fortune and good things abounded. Stripy had hoped for many years, that Finn might find a friend, and now the bee was moved to tears, and hoped that this might be the end. The end of the boy who'd hidden away, the boy who wallowed in pain, who'd never end his suffering, if in the cave he would remain. He'd hidden from himself, hidden from his past, the fears that he had never faced, might now be overcome at last. The fear of being disliked, the fear of humiliation, the fear of being out in the world, and still suffering isolation. The bee was not merely a creature, something soft that flies, it was caring and insightful, the bee was very wise. But never had the bee imagined, that hiding in the cave, Finn might be discovered, and at last he might be saved.

Now breaking from its hesitation, with buzzy bee determination, in swift and purposeful ascent, up towards the roof it went. Other than some figures of eight, its flight path did not deviate, until at some fantastic height, the bee entered the beams of light. The beams of light Myshi had noticed, after she had laughed at Finn, they came from holes in the firmament, from there the light of day came in.

Myshi's heart was full of hope, would the bee throw down a rope? It was a very long way from the ground, she wasn't sure if she could cope.

Finns question had not yet been answered, he did not want Myshi to go, nor did Myshi want to leave, but she knew the answer must be no. She could see that he was still afraid, desperate for her to stay, now that he had made a friend, he wished she would not go away.

She sensed that he already knew, he must say goodbye to Myshi Moo, but she sensed the words might hurt too much, he had no one else to go back to. Around his eyes his eyelids quivered, unsmiling lips appeared to shiver, before Myshi Moo could even speak, he hung his head in quiet defeat.

Into the empty chamber, where Finn and Myshi stood alone, the buzzy bee returned, to take Myshi Moo back home. From an atrium in the roof, Myshi watched something unfold, a never- ending roll, of velvety black and gold. There was still enough illumination, from the fire Finn had kindled, to see their saddened features, though the heat had dwindled. Soft golds and reds and browns, flickered on their faces, the time had come to separate, back to their separate places.

The rolling velvet had descended, it hovered at her knees, and it would be her transportation, made up of countless bees. Myshi knew her time was up, she wished that she could stay, she took another look at Finn, before the bees whisked her away. The frightening face seemed to be fading, hazel eyes stared back at blue, Finn felt a painful sadness, and Myshi felt like crying too.

She smiled bravely but had to go "I'll always be your friend you know."

"Goodbye," he said reluctantly, "will you come back and visit me?"

Before Myshi could answer him, things were set in motion, the cave filled with a rising din, a frantic buzzing commotion. The bees entirely engulfed her, all except her hazel eyes, still upright and motionless, Myshi Moo began to rise.

Finn's undiscovered living space, no longer felt like home, too familiar and foreboding, for years it had been all he'd known. The old place seemed to press on him, as if the walls were closing in. Finn felt like he was sinking, like he was tied with chains, the cave felt like a narrow grave, he called out Myshi's name.

"Myshi! Myshi! Wait for me! I'm coming too, I want to see!" Myshi Moo was paralysed, temporarily, she could not move a muscle, they were held in place by bees. But she had heard what Finn had shouted, her heart turned somersaults, the fact she did not dance with joy, was really not her fault.

She could not even answer him, for fear the bees would all fly in, to any orifice created, and she'd quickly be asphyxiated. But Finn had quelled his reservations, he did not need Myshi's permission, he set of with no hesitation, the boy was on a mission. With the speed of a gazelle, leaping from a lions bite, Finn had run and launched himself, to an extraordinary height.

Myshi's pupils nearly popped, if her jaw could move it

would have dropped, a line of bees swung like a whip, and coiled itself around Finn's hips. The falling boy was reeled back in, immobilised and mummified, wrapped from head to toe in bees, then placed with Myshi, side by side.

If Myshi Moo could turn her head, if she could have seen Finn's face, she could have seen how glad he was, to leave his hiding place. Even though he was afraid, and part of him would wish he'd stayed, the loneliness he'd felt before, was the one thing he could not endure. As long as anybody knew, inside that cave he had remained, can you imagine how he felt, to see the world outside again?

Exiting the secret cave, through the holes from where the light, had frequented his hidden world, gave the frightening face a fright. His experience of the episode, felt like being reborn, delivered to a brand- new life, where he would not be forlorn. Still he could not help himself, he slammed his eyelids closed, it took the poor boy quite a while, until he was composed. Composed enough to take a chance, once he could control his breathing, and brave enough to take a glance, that left him not believing. Not believing all those years, hidden in the cave he'd stayed, living only for revenge, never seeing the light of day. And what a thing the daylight was, a beauty he'd forgotten, hiding from the world so long, he'd become besotten.

As the children had erupted, from the hidden living space, the virgin air and evening sun, awed the frightening face. The landscape and the colours, might make you think of desolation, but for Finn they were astonishing, beyond his starved imagination. Clouds of pink and purple skies, greeted his blue dumbstruck eyes, the golden earth scattered with rocks, almost left the boy shell shocked. They passed a chirping flock of birds, quotidian they sounded, but they were unlike anything he'd heard, the chirping left the boy astounded. The unknown beauty of it all, seemed utterly incredible, the startled child could not stop blinking, his bewildered brain could do no thinking.

With mind and body paralysed, by the bees and what he saw, he could not move nor vocalise, but he was not the boy he'd been before. The flood of information, had caused a rearranging, of something in his brain, the frightening face was changing.

After travelling some distance, the bees relinquished their insistence, on holding solidly in place, Myshi Moo and the frightening face. Finn realised that he could shrug, his shoulders set free by the bugs, he found that he could move his fingers, and the bees had spared him from their stingers. The bees began to tumble off, and form a floor furry and soft, beneath their cargo held aloft, upon whom movement was betrothed. All around the sky seemed vast, Finn gasped an ecstatic gasp, then fell back and gazed about amazed, at the world as it flew past.

The gasp became a happy howl, antithetical to the scowl, the frightening face had always favoured, for untold aeons until now. Giddily he kicked his feet, his transformation near complete, he welcomed with infectious laughter, his new unfolding ever after. The laughter went in all directions, his friend did not escape infection, together they laughed with all their might, on their fantastic buzzing flight.

The barren lands had passed below, replaced by trees that trumpets blow, and greedy grass where few dared go, the million bees began to slow. The travellers had not conversed, great distances they had traversed, though flying less than half an hour, they now approached the green clock towers.

It was evening as the bees went down, they left them near the edge of town, their journey all but at an end, Myshi Moo and her new friend. Not far from where the children were, her parents were expecting her, this time much more patiently, they knew she'd come eventually. What fools they'd been to act with haste, it all had nearly gone to waste, they'd nearly thrown their lives away, but were rescued by the frightening face. Now they sat there gratefully, besides the most amazing tea, all manner of chocolate and delights, if need be they would wait all night.

The grass and flowers undulated, Finn took in their pleasant scent, nobody knew where he would go, after Myshi went. She looked at him and realised, there was no sadness in his eyes, he seemed just like another child, not someone trauma had defiled. He seemed normal, slight of build, independent and strong willed, a boy who'd been a monster, now standing there, in the field. His gait was straight, his features shone, the damaged vengeful boy was gone. His face did not betray emotion; his movements gave no clue, of what the boy was thinking, or what the boy might do.

Over yonder in the town, lights went on as the sun went down, twilight waited for its cue, easterly the shadows flew.

"Well" said Myshi to her friend, "I guess that's it for me. I must say that was quite an adventure, we certainly had fun didn't we?" She'd intended just to say goodbye, and quickly run back home, before Finn saw her crying, at the thought of leaving him alone. She'd go back to her sleepless life, she wondered what she'd do, she knew the tea would be delicious, she wished that Finn could have some too.

But she was sure that he would go, back to his hiding place, and once again he would become, that terrible frightening face. Myshi knew she would be lonely, when she heard other children scream, she'd never see her friend again, because she never dreamed.

A few undetermined steps she took, through the field of flowers, back to her old sleepless life, in the town with green clock towers. The boy who'd been the frightening face, did not say goodbye, he stood silently and watched her go, Myshi saw in her mind's eye. She kept her focus straight ahead, her home was in the distance, she urged her feet to keep moving, despite her hearts resistance.

"Don't look back, don't look back," she whispered quietly to herself, the evening sky was turning black, and she wished that she was someone else. Not the girl whose heart was breaking, not the girl who never slept, as she got closer to her home, Myshi quietly wept. She had chocolate to consume, she was headed home for tea, her parents would be overjoyed, so she tried to feel happy.

Before much longer she was gone, the field of flowers left behind, the memories of what she had seen, securely locked up in her mind. Back amongst the houses, she could see her own front door, when the light from someone's window, cast a shadow on the floor. Somebody was behind her, stalking silently, Myshi felt that her adventure, might end violently. The fear raised Myshi's heart rate, it made her jump and spin, to face the danger that she sensed, and she saw that it was Finn. Finn had followed her from the field, Myshi tried to speak, Finn carefully used his thumbs, to wipe the tears from Myshi's cheeks. He put his finger on her lips, to stop Myshi from talking, he smiled reassuringly, then took her hand and kept on walking.

About the Author

Nasar Karim was born and raised in London. He has also lived in Poland. Currently his favourite country is Norway. After graduating from the University of Kent at Canterbury, he ran his own businesses for ten years whilst thinking he'd rather be a writer or a musician. Another ten years later, he realised he still wanted to be an author and completed his first book. When he's not writing or doing his day job, Nasar can be found listening to old bands, playing music, reading, lifting weights, or having a good time.

Acknowledgements

Myshi Moo and The Frightening Face could not have been written without the support of my wife. A special thanks must go to my daughters who gave me the impetus to get started and provided inspiration for the characters. Finally I must acknowledge my friends, Ted Burke, Alan Quadling, and Qaisir Shabir. The story of Myshi Moo would never have been completed without their feedback and encouragement.